H.O.T. Faith

Hearing, Obeying and Trusting

Nancy Goudie

Sovereign World

Sovereign World Ltd
PO Box 777
Tonbridge
Kent TN11 0ZS
England

ISBN 1 85240 379 9

Cover design by CCD, www.ccdgroup.co.uk
Typeset by CRB Associates, Reepham, Norfolk
Printed in England by Clays Ltd, St Ives plc

Dedication

This book is dedicated to those who have encouraged and strengthened me in my own personal journey of faith.

Ken and Hazel McGreavy, Ian Andrews, Ian Leitch, Smith Wigglesworth, Colin Urquhart, my parents Jack and Mary McVicar, my husband and my closest friend Ray, all Heartbeaties and ngmers past and present, and all those who have stood with Ray and me and prayed, fasted and sacrificially given to us over the years – this book is for you.

Contents

Acknowledgments

I am extremely grateful for the help and encouragement I have received from the following people. Without their love, care and sacrifice, I would not have been able to write this book.

First of all to my husband and best friend, Ray, whose constant encouragement, creativity, wisdom, advice and much more throughout this project, have kept me on the right track. Ray, thank you so much for the practical help you gave me in taking over some of my roles in the house whilst I was writing. Thank you for proof reading the book for me and for the helpful insight and comments you gave. But most of all thank you for the way you inspire faith in me by not being afraid to be out on a limb for God. My faith in God has grown enormously over the years we have been married because of your example of daily faith in a living and active God. We have walked through so many scary yet exciting journeys of faith together. I am so grateful to God that we have had each other to share our adventure of faith.

To all our faithful supporters who have sacrificially given finance and practical help to us throughout the years to enable us to do the work that God has called us to do. You truly are partners with us in this work. We will forever be grateful to you. Thank you for your special friendship.

To June, Zoe, and Ally who are in my admin support team, and to Suse who joins the team to pray with me every week – all of you have been such an encouragement to me. Thank you for your friendships, encouragement, prayers and practical help.

To Sarah Lowe who works part-time in the marketing side of ngm. Thank you so much for proof reading the book for me and for your very helpful comments and encouragement.

To Becca and Helen for helping me with Aidan – without your practical help this book would not have been written.

To Daniel, my teenage son – the way you live your life and the way you demonstrate your faith in God is such an inspiration.

To Aidan, my six-year-old son – your simple faith in God and the way you communicate that to others is wonderful.

To Tim Pettingale for believing in me and this project. It is great to work with you and all at Sovereign World.

To all our intercessors who have soaked this project in prayer – I can never thank you enough for praying for me and for us as a family.

To my Dad and to the memory of my Mum – both of you have infected my life with the love and joy of Jesus. I will eternally be grateful for the years where you taught me what it means to demonstrate faith in a mighty God.

And finally to my Heavenly Father. How can I ever thank You enough for the way You have watched me and kept me throughout the years. Thank You for encouraging me to keep going through all the tough times and for continuing to teach me what it means to live by faith.

About the Author

Nancy Goudie, along with her husband Ray, has been in full-time Christian ministry since 1980. She became a Christian when, at the age of six, she had a very dramatic and powerful experience of God. During the first twenty-two years of her life, she attended a Brethren church in her hometown of Ayr, Scotland. During her teens she became part of a well-established Christian band called Unity. As well as singing with the band, she also put her qualifications in speech (Associate of the London College of Music) to good use by being one of the narrators in the musicals that Unity produced.

Ray and Nancy left Scotland in 1980 with a vision from God to start a ministry through which God could reach the youth of their land. In 1981, Ray and Nancy founded and led the internationally known band Heartbeat. As one of the singers and main speakers, she travelled and ministered throughout the UK and abroad and saw a mighty move of God's Spirit with many young people being touched by the power of God and swept into the Kingdom.

Towards the end of the '80s they changed the overall name of their ministry to ngm (new generation music and mission) with Heartbeat being one of their bands. Although Heartbeat finished in 1991, Nancy's gifts of preaching and teaching have continued to be used through the ministry of ngm not only in Britain but also in mainland Europe and the USA. Her passion and love for Jesus is evident to all who meet her. She has also been interviewed on radio and television numerous times about her faith in God and has a regular show called *A Slice of Life* on UCB radio.

Nancy and Ray now have over 120 full-time people working with them in evangelism, church planting, music, mission and training and they have seen thousands of people in Britain and abroad come into a vibrant living relationship with the Lord Jesus. Both individually and corporately they live by faith and have seen God provide for their ministry in miraculous ways over and over again. In 2001 they completed a huge walk of faith, having seen God release £3 million to purchase and build a missions and arts centre in Thornbury, near Bristol, England, where they are based.

Nancy has written five books as well as many articles for magazines and newspapers. She has also recorded three powerful meditation CDs through which many have come into a deeper and more intimate walk with Jesus.

Nancy and her husband Ray have two sons, Daniel (16) and Aidan (6).

To find out more about Nancy and the work she does, visit her website at www.nancygoudie.com.

What Others Are Saying About H.O.T Faith . . .

'Nancy Goudie knows that our God is living and active, answering prayer and performing miracles today as surely as he did two thousand years ago. Nancy knows it because the Bible promises it, but she also knows it from personal experience. She is a hero of faith. Whatever mountains you need to move, this remarkable book will build your faith and empower your prayers. Best of all, it will help you to grow in faithfulness as a friend of God.'   *Pete Greig, 24/7 Prayer*

'There is nothing like a good story of what God has done to help build our faith – and Nancy Goudie is full of them! I know, because I walked through many of them with her and her husband, Ray.'
                                                      Andy Hunter, DJ

'One of the greatest joys in my life is when my son runs to do what I ask him to do whether it makes sense to him or not. Those moments are rare! If that kind of pure faith means so much to a mum I can't begin to imagine what it means to our heavenly Father when we run to do whatever He asks us to do simply because we love and trust Him. In this book my good friend, Nancy, takes us on the great adventure of what it looks like to live that way. It's a journey that could change your life forever.'   *Sheila Walsh, singer and songwriter*

'This book is a testimony that "we walk by faith, not by sight." When we do what we can, God will do what we can't. Faith is not believing that God can – it's knowing that He will. Be inspired in your own journey as you read this book.'   *Canon J. John, Philo Trust*

'If you want to climb mountains, ask a mountaineer. If you want to paint great paintings, ask an artist. It is a simple but very effective life principle – always consult someone who knows because they have done it. That's why if you want to learn about faith, real faith, life transforming faith, one of my suggestions would be to talk to Nancy Goudie. This book lets you do just that and, I guarantee, will grip you from the first story to the last.'   *Steve Chalke,*
                        Founder Oasis Trust and Faithworks

'I have known Nancy and her husband, Ray for many years. They really do walk the walk not just talk the talk. I've seen first-hand the miraculous provision of God for their lives and ministry as they've continually launched out on the high wire of faith with God.'

Graham Kendrick, *worship leader and songwriter*

'A fantastic read – what a sizzler!' **Mike Pilavachi**, *Soul Survivor*

'God calls all His children to live by faith. The way to do this is first to listen to those who have done it themselves! – those who have dared to trust God and proved His faithfulness to His words and promises. This book will inspire you to trust Him and see the way in which He provides for you.' **Colin Urquhart**, *Kingdom Faith*

'Nancy's book encourages people to listen and obey. It reminds us that faith should be outworked in everyday life.'

Rob Frost, *Share Jesus International*

Introduction

'You want to do what? Contact my brother and ask him to give us his car? No way, Ray – you will start a family row.' I could not believe what I was hearing . . .

We had a car that had been our faithful friend for many years, but it was no longer suitable for the many thousands of miles we travelled. When we went to God in prayer about it, the first thing He said to us was 'Give your car away and I will provide for you.' So after praying and talking things through together, we approached someone who was working with us in Heartbeat at the time. When we told him and his wife that we were giving them our car it was a complete answer to prayer for them. They had been praying that God would supply them with a car. After obeying what God had said, we then went back to God with renewed passion saying 'OK God, we've told Jack and Susan we are giving our car away . . . so now where is our car?'

After Ray and I had prayed for some time, we decided to pray separately and come together to hear what we felt God was saying to us both. When Ray told me he got a verse of scripture from God, I got really excited. He then took me to a passage in Luke 19 where Jesus asked His disciples to go and collect a donkey for Him. Jesus told them that if someone asked them why they were taking the donkey they should say, *'The Lord needs it'* (Luke 19:34). Ray then lifted his head from the Bible and said 'Nancy, I believe we should phone your brother, Jim, and tell him "The Lord has need of your car, Jim." '

I could not believe the words that were coming out of Ray's mouth. Ask my brother for his car? Surely God was not asking us to do that. After I had calmed down, Ray said to me, 'Look, I don't know if I have heard correctly from God, but there is one thing I would ask you to do. Would you pray and ask God if this word is from Him, and if you come back to me and say that you do not witness the word, then we will forget it. On the other hand, if you come back saying that it is a word from God, then we can discuss what we should do.'

I immediately felt relieved. There was no way that this could possibly be a word from God. I just needed to pray and ask God to confirm that it was wrong and everything would be fine. However, after I spent some time praying and laying down my preconceived ideas, I had to come back to Ray and say that I felt this was indeed a word from God. I couldn't believe what we were going to do. I could just imagine what my family would say. Never before had I ever phoned my brothers and asked them for anything, never mind a car.

My brother, who is a Baptist pastor, was moving from his home and pastorate in Poole in Dorset to be a minister of a church in the States. When I plucked up enough courage to phone him, he immediately said he had been about to phone us. I took a deep breath and said, 'Jim ... ' and there was a big pause. I then quickly said, 'Ray wants to speak to you!' As I handed the phone to a very surprised Ray, I mouthed to Ray – 'I can't ask him!' Ray took the phone and bravely said, 'Jim, we were just wondering what you were doing with your car since you are moving to the States?' Jim replied, 'Are you interested in buying it? I could give you a great price on it if you wish?' As Ray stumbled over his next few words, Jim added, 'Pray about it and let me know if you and Nancy want the car.'

As Ray and I put the phone down we had a great sadness in our hearts, as we knew we had not done what God had asked us to do. We had not told Jim, 'The Lord has need of it'. The next day we were off on holiday to Weston-super-Mare. Now, I must say there is nothing wrong with Weston-super-Mare, nor with the fantastic cottage that had been loaned to us by some friends, but it was the worst holiday of my life! Every day, as we spent time with the Lord, He would say to us, 'You haven't done what I asked you to do'. By the end of an agonising week, Ray and I went home determined to do what God had told us to do. We knew we had to phone Jim and tell him, 'The Lord has need of your car' despite the possibility of family eruptions and being totally misunderstood.

When we got home I said, 'Ray, you phone Jim and I will back you in prayer!' I still felt I could not physically ask my brother so while poor Ray lifted the telephone, this woman of 'great' faith went upstairs to our bedroom and closed the door. I could not bear even to hear a little of what Ray was saying on the phone. So as I got down on my knees before God I put my hands over my ears and started to pray to God in a loud voice! I interceded like I had never interceded before. My prayer went something like this, 'God – please *help* us!'

Ray plucked up his courage and picked up the phone and when Jim answered he quickly said, 'Look, Jim, when we phoned you last week, Nancy and I did not tell you what we felt God had said to us. We felt God tell us to phone you and say, 'The Lord has need of your car.' Jim immediately responded by saying, 'That's great, Ray – you can have it.'

Jim began to explain what had been happening with him and his wife, Anne. Before we had phoned the first time, they had been praying and felt that they should give their car to us. They were just about to phone us when we called. When Jim came off the phone Anne asked him why he hadn't given the car to us and he explained that 'something' had held him back and he had begun to have doubts as to whether it was right to give us the car. After the phone call and throughout the next week, Jim had tried everything to sell his car. He had advertised it in his church, in the newspapers and on the radio and although this was at a time when second-hand cars where selling very quickly, he didn't even have one enquiry about it.

At the end of the week Jim had said to Anne that he just needed
one more confirmation that it was right to give the car to us. It
was at that point that Ray phoned to say 'The Lord has need of
your car, Jim.' You can imagine our excitement at the end of
that phone call. God had answered our prayers but we just
wished we had put our faith into action the week before and
saved ourselves a week of sheer agony.

We learned a huge lesson in faith that day. Listening to God
is good but better still is listening and obeying. There is a little
verse in James which says,

> *'Do not merely listen to the word ... Do what it says.'*
> (James 1:22)

That verse says it all. We must not only hear what God is
saying; we must also put our faith into action and obey God. I
am sure that the Lord held Jim back from giving us the car to
see if we would obey Him despite the circumstances.

It was only after our faith-journey that we realised that we
did not even know what kind of car my brother Jim had. It
could have been a small mini for all we knew. In the end it
turned out to be a beautiful Saab with only a few thousand
miles on the clock and a front seat which heated up! God is so
amazing. He gives great gifts to His children.

The principle of listening and obeying God is something we
can see in action many times throughout the Bible. It was only
as Esther put her trust in God and went in to see the king that
her prayers were answered and her nation was saved. It was
only as Naaman dipped himself in the river Jordon seven times
that he was healed. It was only as Martha obeyed God and
allowed Lazarus' grave to be opened up that a miracle occurred.
All of them could quite easily have refused, but in order to see
their miracles happen, they needed to put their faith and
obedience into action.

Many years ago I heard a true story about an acrobat named
Blondin who used to perform amazing feats such as crossing
the Niagara Falls on a tightrope, usually without having a

safety net. One day he decided to try and push a wheelbarrow carrying a heavy sack of cement across the tightrope. As the crowds watched him they knew that if he put one foot wrong he would plunge to his death. A roar of appreciation came from the crowd as he reached the other side. One reporter from a newspaper approached him and said, 'Mr. Blondin that was fantastic! You are absolutely amazing!' Blondin said thank you and then asked the reporter, 'Do you believe I can do anything on a tightrope?' The reporter excitedly said, 'Yes I certainly do. I know you can do anything.' Blondin then said, 'Well if you believe that I can do anything, what if I told you that instead of taking this bag of cement across the falls I could put a man inside the wheelbarrow and wheel him across? Do you believe that I could do that?' The reporter said, 'Yes I certainly do believe you can do it!' Blondin said to the reporter, 'Jump in then!' The reporter ran a mile; you could not see him for dust.

You see believing is not enough. The devil and the whole demonic realm believe in God. We must go further than just believing, we must actually jump into the wheelbarrow and go out on a limb for God. In other words we must activate our faith and obey God – then we can expect to receive what God has promised.

After the reporter had disappeared, however, one very courageous person volunteered to sit in the wheelbarrow and go across the Niagara Falls with Blondin. As they got ready to proceed on their momentous journey, people started placing bets on the outcome.

Would he make it? Would he accomplish it or would they both plunge to their deaths? You can imagine how nervous the passenger was as Blondin took his first steps onto the tightrope. The passenger had put all his faith and trust in Blondin's ability to keep him alive.

About halfway across it looked very likely that those who had believed in Blondin's ability were going to win the bet. But a man who had a heavy bet against Blondin succeeding, decided to take the matter into his own hands. He crept over to the wires and cut one of them. As he did so, suddenly the

tightrope whipped back and forth. Blondin fought to keep his
balance, knowing that they were only a few seconds from
death. He knew that if the rim of the wheelbarrow came off the
rope, then they would both plunge to their deaths. As you can
imagine, the passenger was frozen with fright. Blondin shouted
to him, 'Quick! Stand up and grab onto me!' But the man
remained frozen to the spot. Blondin shouted again to him,
'Let go of the wheelbarrow. Stand up now. Do it or die!' The
man suddenly realised that he had to move and obey Blondin
in order to be saved. Somehow the man managed to stir up the
courage to stand up. Blondin told him to put his arms around
his neck and his legs around his waist. As the man obeyed,
the empty wheelbarrow fell into the swirling waters below.
Blondin stood there using every muscle in his body to keep
him and his passenger on the wire until the wire stopped
swaying back and forth. Then inch-by-inch he made his way
safely across to the other side.

Blondin's passenger that day displayed real faith. He not
only believed in Blondin, but he was willing to put his faith
into action. During his faith experience, he knew that in order
to survive he had to continue to put his faith into action and
obey Blondin's every instruction. As he did so he became like a
little child hugging his father. As he continued to hug tightly,
he saw what Blondin had promised come into being.

In every area of our lives God wants us to react in a similar
manner. It is important that we don't just believe that God *can*
do it, but that we put our faith and obedience into action and
step out on that high wire with God. Every faith walk is an
exciting and yet sometimes scary experience and there will
be times when you know that unless God steps in, you will be
dead. It is so important in those times that we not only listen
but also obey God's every instruction. When we 'hug' God and
cling to Him on the high wire, He will somehow bring us safely
to the other side.

My prayer is that this book, which is full of true stories of
faith, will encourage you and fuel your passion to 'live by
faith' in every area of your lives. This does not mean that this

book is only for those who are in full-time Christian work and who depend on God for finances. God wants each of us, whether we have a salary or not, to live by faith and not by sight and to see Him accomplish the miraculous in our every-day circumstances.

This book is not just filled with *teaching* on the subject of faith; it is also full of true and inspiring stories of how faithful our God is. Many of the stories have come from my husband, Ray and myself as we have walked in faith with God throughout the many years we have been in 'full-time' Christian work. It contains the story of how Heartbeat/ngm came into being and the amazing things God did throughout our first ten years in Christian work when we led the Heartbeat band. It reveals how our work has grown and developed and how we saw God provide for us a £3 million missions and arts centre as our base. I have tried to be accurate in every story, please forgive me though if my memory has failed me over any detail. I have tried to be as honest as I can in each story so that you will see our 'pain' as well as our joy, so that you can see our failures as well as our successes.

You will see threaded throughout each chapter three steps that need to be taken in order to live a faith-filled life and develop 'hot faith'. The first is Hearing God; the second is Obeying God and the third is Trusting God.

Hearing ...

Obeying ...   **God**

Trusting ...

When you combine these steps, watch out for a miracle!

At the end of every chapter I have written study notes along with creative spiritual exercises so that you can get into the wheelbarrow, learn to 'hug' God on the high wire and live a life of intimacy, obedience and faith. These exercises can be done alone or with others.

May the teaching of this book and the true stories contained within it fuel your faith and fire your passion for God so that you can truly have red 'hot faith'. Go for it and enjoy your journey of faith.

Nancy Goudie

Chapter 1

Beginnings of Faith

> I opened the envelope and there inside were four ten pound postal orders – exactly the amount I needed.

In 1978, my husband, Ray, had been invited to be part of a band that a singer/speaker called Dave Pope was putting together for a tour that would last six months. Ray was thrilled to be invited, but as he was working in his parents' shoe-retail business, it meant him asking if he could have six months leave of absence. At first the answer was no and although Ray was deeply disappointed he went back to Dave and his musical director, John Daniels, and told them that it was impossible for him to drum in the band. I was so disappointed for Ray, but as I prayed about it I felt that it was right for him to be involved, so I prayed that somehow God would allow it to happen.

A few weeks later we received another phone call from John and Dave saying that each time they prayed about a drummer for the band, God kept bringing Ray's name to their mind. They asked if Ray would go back to his parents and ask again. We prayed that if it was right that Ray's parents would change their minds and allow Ray to have the time off work. Thankfully, Ray's parents love the Lord Jesus and said they would pray and ask God about it. Whilst praying, they felt if three certain conditions were met then they would give a positive answer. The first condition was that Ray should only go for five months and come home after the Canadian part of the tour. The second condition was that one of the ladies who worked in the shop would have to be prepared to work full-time during that period. The third was that I was happy that Ray would be away from me for three weeks at a time – I would only possibly see him one week in four. I was extremely positive that it was the right thing for him to do, the shop assistant agreed to do the extra hours and John and Dave said they would bring in another drummer for the last month of the tour.

Before we knew it, Ray was off on tour with what turned out to be a great bunch of people. The keyboard player in the band was Chris Eaton who is now a singer-songwriter in his own right. He has penned thousands of fantastic songs, many of which have been sung by people such as Cliff Richard, Amy Grant, and Sheila Walsh. The most well known one was the hit by Cliff Richard, 'Saviours' Day'. The acoustic guitarist was Ian White who is now widely known for leading worship and for his Psalms recordings. On lead guitar was Rob Marshall who for some time was in the Mark Williamson Band in the '80s. His wife, Liz, was also there to help with admin and stock. We were already close friends with singer- songwriter John Daniels who was on bass guitar. Each person in the band has now become a special friend and our friendships have lasted down the years. God did so much in each of the band members during those six months and we are so grateful to God and to Dave Pope for bringing us all together. It was during those six months that God called Ray and myself to leave our jobs and become missionaries for Him.

During the first couple of months, whilst Ray was drumming for Dave at an event in Norwich, Ray met a young singer called Graham Kendrick. As Graham chatted to Ray, Ray was amazed to hear Graham ask him if he had ever thought of going into full-time Christian work. When Ray said that the thought had never entered his mind, Graham then encouraged him to pray about it. He revealed that he had been feeling from God during the day that God's call was on Ray's life.

As the weeks went by more and more people kept asking Ray

and myself if we had ever considered working for God. Although I realised that it would take a miracle to get Ray to move from Scotland, when I prayed about our future I felt God confirm to me that we would at some point be in full-time work for God. At the very first Spring Harvest, Eric Delve, who was the national evangelist with British Youth for Christ at the time, took time out of his busy schedule to sit us down and tell us that he believed God was calling us.

At that same camp, God broke into my husband's life in a way that totally changed him and his direction. I have told the story in my book *Nancy Goudie's Spiritual Health Workout* of how eight months before going on tour with Dave, Ray came to a crisis in his life. He announced to me one day that he was giving up his Christian faith and that although he didn't mind if I went to church, he no longer wished to be involved in any Christian activity. He explained that he had been living in defeat as a Christian and therefore no longer wanted to live as a hypocrite. He remembered when he was nine, laughing as he and his brother went forward at a meeting to give their lives to Christ. That incident had always bothered him and put doubts in his mind about his faith. Perhaps he was not a Christian? He understood that when you became a Christian you received the Holy Spirit and therefore would have power in your life. As he had no power and was living in defeat, he wrongly reckoned that he did not have the Holy Spirit. He then concluded he could not be a Christian!

As you can imagine, I was devastated. I knew that if Ray went in one direction and I in another then that would be the end of our marriage. I loved Ray with every fibre of my being and so I poured out my heart to God for him. Have you ever gone through times in your prayer life when you felt that God was not listening? To me, that day heaven seemed closed. My every prayer seemed to hit the ceiling. After crying myself to sleep that night, I started again to pray for Ray the next morning. I was determined to keep on praying until somehow God answered. At that time in our lives, I was only working for three hours each day and so I spent all morning bombarding heaven with my prayers and tears. When I went to work though, I could hardly disguise my distress. The first thing I did after work was to get down on my knees again and plead with God to do something in Ray.

Around five o'clock that night, God answered. If He had spoken in an audible voice, I could not have heard Him more clearly. He told me 'Nancy, I have heard your prayers and I have seen your tears. Don't cry anymore because if you could see what I am going to do in Ray, you would not believe it. Instead of praying for Ray, begin to praise Me for what I am about to do.' My tears and prayers were suddenly transformed into praise and dancing. I danced up and down our lounge knowing without a doubt that God had spoken and all would be okay. Hearing from God is of huge importance in our lives. This is the first step to living an exciting faith-filled life. When God speaks, true faith is kindled in our hearts. That day God showed me again just how important it is to listen to Him through His written Word and also through His still small voice.

When Ray came in from work a couple of minutes later, I could not contain my excitement and told him all that God had said. A cold look came across his face as he told me that if God had spoken then *He* was going to have to do it as he felt exactly the same and still did not want anything to do with Christianity.

Unknown to Ray, I started to praise God daily for what God was going to do in him. There were times throughout the next number of months when I got impatient and even angry with God. Why was nothing happening? Why was I not seeing a change in Ray? I remember one night, whilst Ray was sound asleep beside me, hitting my pillow in frustration and shouting at God, 'When Lord? When are You going to do what You have said You would do?' It was only in retrospect that I realised that from the moment God spoke from heaven, He had started to work behind the scenes. I could not see Him working, but that did not mean God was being idle.

When Ray had been invited to be part of Dave's tour, this was the glimmer of hope I needed to encourage me in my prayers. Ray had reckoned he was okay going on Dave's tour because he could hide behind the drums. Dave had explained that this would be an evangelistic tour, however after a couple of nights Dave suddenly changed his message from evangelism to begin to challenge the Christians in the audience to live a vibrant life in Christ. Each night Ray heard God speak directly into his heart. He began again to read his Bible and to study the Bible with Rob and Liz Marshall. I noticed the tone of his letters and postcards beginning to change as God was working in his life.

When he got to Spring Harvest, Luis Palau (the Argentinean evangelist) spoke from the following verse in 2 Corinthians.

> 'We always carry around in our body the death of Jesus, so that the life of Jesus may also be revealed in our body.'
> (2 Corinthians 4:10)

He told his own story of how he would pray and dedicate his life to Christ every Sunday but then by the following Friday he would blow it. He would then rededicate his life to God again and again he would blow it. This continued to happen until someone took him aside and explained 2 Corinthians 4:10 and asked him if he wanted to be victorious in his Christian life and no longer keep swaying from victory to defeat. Luis told us that he had revelation of what it meant to be obedient to Christ. He said that every time God's will crossed his will, he went God's way and not his own way not only in the big issues of life but also in the small areas. This decision of the will changed his life. Ray was challenged by what Luis had said and reckoned, 'If it is good enough for Luis Palau, then it is good enough for me.' I remember Ray, with tears in his eyes, telling me that God had spoken to him and he was now going to live for Jesus.

Just after Spring Harvest, Ray went to Canada on a six-week trip that was supposed to take in a tour of the States as well. Just before they left for Canada, the American part of the tour fell through which left Ray and the rest of the band with nothing to do for four weeks. However, it was during those four weeks that God cemented the change in Ray. Each day, Ray put into practice what he had learned from Luis. Ray would say to God, 'What do You want me to do today?' And whatever God said, Ray had already made up his mind that he would do.

In the Bible, when the Israelites were building Jerusalem, we read in Nehemiah that Ezra gathered all the people to hear the Law (the Bible of their day) being read. In Nehemiah 8:6, it tells us that the people said *'Amen, Amen'* (which means 'So, let it be') before they knew what God was going to say. In other words they were saying 'Whatever You say, Lord. Whatever You ask us to do we will obey You.' It is so important in our lives to determine to be obedient to the will of God. As we obey, God releases His power to help us to do His will.

Similar to the Israelites, Ray had made up his mind to obey God in the small things in life as well as in the big decisions he had to make. Each day he would be obedient and read his Bible and pray. One morning, when he read in the Bible that he needed to be filled with the Holy Spirit, he went down on his knees and asked the Lord to fill him with His Spirit. There were no flashes from the sky, but Ray knew within himself that God had done what he had asked Him to do. Certainly when I saw him several weeks later, I saw the difference in him for myself.

In the second week of his time in Canada, shortly after praying and asking God what He wanted him to do that day, he received a phone call from someone who asked him if he would be a volunteer to help build a ranch for a Christian organisation. Although Ray's natural reaction would have been to say no, he felt it was right to say yes. In order to get to the ranch he had to travel several miles on a bus. During his journey he noticed that a girl sitting in the seat in front of him was crying. He felt God nudge him and ask him to speak to her. Again choosing to go God's way, he nervously asked her if she was okay. She told Ray that she had run away from a children's home and a social worker was bringing her back. Ray spoke to her and told her about the love of God. She listened to all that he had to say and before leaving the bus, she agreed to meet with some Christians that Ray knew who 'just happened' to live in her town.

When he arrived at the ranch, Ray was given the job of digging the sewers! He could not believe it. His complaints to God went something like this: 'Lord, I am a drummer! Drummers don't dig sewers!' But because he had said he would always put God's will first, he said he would do it. The next morning, Ray was thrilled to see that it was pouring with rain. He reckoned he would not have to dig the sewers today because it was so wet and he didn't have a raincoat! He was wrong! They provided him with boots, a coat and a hat that were all too big for him and sent him out in the pouring rain. As he dug the sewers, I am sure God must have smiled from heaven. Ray discovered, however, that even when he was soaked through to the skin there was a joy about doing what God had told him to do.

When he got back to Toronto, he and a couple of friends, Terry and Ginny Bridle, went to People's Church to a meeting where Brother Andrew was speaking. At the appeal, there was a word of knowledge given that there was someone in the audience who was under 30 years of age who thought God *could* be calling him to work for Him, but did not know *where* God was calling him. Ray knew he was that person. The thought of having to stand in a meeting where 2,000 people were gathered was very intimidating, however because he had made up his mind to obey, he nervously stood. They called him to the front with hundreds of others who had responded to Brother Andrew's message.

On his way out of the church, a man approached Ray and asked him if he felt called to full-time Christian work. When Ray confirmed that this was so, the man went on to say, 'I felt God ask me to come and speak to you. Many years ago, God called me to give up my job and work for Him but because I was involved in my family business and I didn't want to let my parents down; I gave in to family pressure and didn't respond to God's calling. Now, twenty-five years later, I realise I disobeyed God. If this applies to you in any way, do not allow parental pressures to hold you back from what God wants to do with you.' Ray couldn't believe it, as it described his situation so clearly. This was the first and only time this man had met Ray and he had no idea of Ray's background. Ray knew that God was calling him, but he was so worried about what his parents would say if he were to leave the family business. At that point in time, Ray's mum and dad were in the process of changing some of the shares in the business into Ray's name. However, Ray knew that God was speaking and that if he didn't do what God had told him to do, he would be living in disobedience. He gave in to God that night and told Him that no matter what storms would occur, he would obey Him. Ray surrendered his future to God and gave Him control of the whole of his life.

At 11.00 pm that night Ray phoned me, totally forgetting the fact that it was 4.00 am in Scotland. However, when he told me what had happened and how God had totally changed his life, I didn't mind at all being woken out of my sleep, in fact I was thrilled. When I came off the phone that night, I thanked God for answering my prayers and for all He had done in Ray. When I looked in my diary to see when I had started praying and praising God for Ray, I was amazed to discover that it was exactly a year to the day that God had told me He would change my husband's life.

When I met Ray in Canada several days later, I felt like God had given me a new husband! I was truly amazed at what He had done. As it says in the Psalms,

> 'The LORD is faithful to all his promises
> and loving towards all he has made.'   (Psalm 145:13)

Can I encourage you to continue to pray and believe God for a miracle even if you are not at this time seeing God answer your prayers in the way you would like? God will indeed bring His promises into being, and even now will be working behind the scenes to make sure His will is accomplished.

During that early morning phone call, Ray asked me to bring

£50 when I went to Canada in a few days time. He explained that his money was running out and in fact for most of the time that he had been in Toronto, he had been living on a very small McDonalds hamburger and a small carton of milk for his main meal. It was only after I got off the phone, that I started to think to myself, 'How am I going to get £50?' Unknown to Ray, finances were in short supply at home too. We had received several bills at once and I really didn't have any cash to take with me. Before going back to sleep, I remembered that a retired minister had given me £10 to take to Ray while he was in Canada. So, I thought to myself, that means I have to find £40. I said a quick prayer, 'Lord would You somehow provide £40 for me?' The very next morning, when the post came I noticed a hand-written envelope from London. As Ray and I didn't know anyone in London at the time, I was intrigued to find out who could possibly be writing to us. As I opened the envelope, out fell four £10 postal orders made out to me. I could not believe it. I fell to my knees and with tears coming down my face I thanked God for His amazing love and grace to me. This was the first time I had ever seen God provide finance for us – little did I realise that it would be the first of many.

Exercises for your faith muscles

Hearing, obedience and trust are three very important ingredients in any faith walk.

▶ One of the ways of *hearing* God speak to us and encouraging intimacy is through the reading of the Bible. Write down/discuss how important reading the Bible is to you. Think through/discuss ways of reading the Bible and how to prioritise it.

▶ Read 2 Kings 5:1–14. Note that Naaman is asked to do something that he doesn't want to do, but he must be *obedient* in order to see a miracle happen. Analyse your response, if God asked you to do something that you thought was beneath you, that hit at your pride or that was just not 'you'.

▶ Write down an example from the New Testament where Jesus supernaturally provides for a need. Write down/ discuss a time when God has supernaturally provided for you. If He hasn't as yet, then think through/discuss ways of *trusting* God for a new adventure of faith and ask God for the first step.

▶ Memorise Romans 10:17:

> 'Consequently, faith comes from hearing the message, and the message is heard through the word of Christ.'

Chapter 2

Faith for the Future

> 'Don't worry about your loved ones; I will take care of them. You follow after Me.'

When we came home from Canada, Ray gently explained to his parents what God had said and told them he was leaving the business and going into full-time Christian work. Although there had been signs along the way during the five months that Ray had been working with Dave Pope, I'm sure his parents never thought for one moment that Ray would actually leave. Ray wanted to honour his Mum and Dad and so made the decision that he would not move out of the business for a year. He told his parents that by 1st June 1980 we would be moving, even though at that point we had no idea of where we would be going. Ray's Mum and Dad were devastated and the pressure on us to stay was enormous. It was one of the hardest things Ray has ever had to do. It would have been much easier for us to succumb to the pressure to stay in Scotland, but we knew that no matter what, we could not.

Shortly after we arrived home from Canada, we received a phone call from Clive Calver who was the National Director of British Youth for Christ. He asked if he could come and speak to us about the possibility of us joining British Youth for Christ. Little did we know at the time that his visit was going to be very significant for us. During the day he spent with us, we took some time to pray about our future and it was during this prayer session that Clive gave us a prophecy. What he did not realise at the time was that Ray and I had never heard a prophecy in our lives before. When Clive was giving the prophecy I thought to myself, 'This is God.' Ray, however, was much more sceptical. Afterwards I said to Ray, 'Wasn't that amazing?' Ray retorted back, 'Well, if that was God, I'd like Him to confirm His word.' One of the things God said through the prophecy was, 'Do not worry about your loved ones, I will look after them; you follow after Me.' Psalm 37:4–6 was also quoted in the prophecy.

The very next morning after Ray had gone to work, a letter arrived from a friend called Howard Drysdale who was in the merchant navy. The letter had been written several weeks before, but in it he said, 'Ray, I feel I need to stop what I am saying and tell you something I believe God wants you to hear; in fact He may have told you this already.' He went on to quote the prophecy almost word for word and even used the same scriptures. I picked up the phone and called Ray. I read out what was written in the letter and asked him what he thought it was. He said, 'That's the prophecy Clive gave us.' I replied, 'No, it's not. I am reading from a letter we have just received from Howard.' Ray and I were so pleased that God had confirmed the prophecy in such a special way. The Lord knew that Ray needed Him to continue to confirm over and over again that He wanted us to obey Him and that He would look after our loved ones.

Ray and I then decided to take our call to our church leadership. I was particularly nervous about doing that because I wasn't sure how they would respond. As Ray and I shared our hearts and our call, we were astonished at the response from our pastor and the whole eldership team. Some of them were in tears; others had huge smiles and all of them confirmed, including one person who didn't believe that prophetic words were for today that this was indeed God and that we had to obey. They prayed with us and told us they would support us in any way they could. We did not realise that our partnership would last with the majority of these people for many, many years.

We continued to receive confirmation after confirmation as the months went by, but although Ray was 90% sure that God had called us he was still waiting for that extra 10%. I couldn't understand it. We had been receiving confirmation through scripture, through others, through our church leadership and through the peace in our hearts. What more could Ray be looking for? Ray explained that he knew how much our decision was hurting his Mum and Dad and he just needed to be 100% sure.

We went to see a lovely old couple in our church, George and Peggy Kerr, and explained our whole call in great detail. After Ray was finished, George turned to Ray and asked him what he was waiting for. Ray responded by explaining that he was 90% sure but he still wanted to have that extra 10% confirmation. George wisely said, 'Maybe the 10% extra you need is you exercising your faith and jumping into God's plan for your life. There always has to be a certain amount of faith and obedience expressed on our part in every faith walk. You exercise your faith and the 10% will be there.' We left with joy in our hearts, knowing that if we obeyed and put our faith into action, God would take care of us and our loved ones.

A year later, our church commissioned us and sent us out as their missionaries. They asked Clive Calver to come and speak at our valedictory service, which they arranged in May 1980. The day of the service just so happened to be the day when, two years previously, God had promised to change my husband's life and had told me that if I could 'see it now, I would not believe it'. As we knelt that day to be prayed for by the elders, tears poured down my face as I remembered the goodness and faithfulness of God. If God had not intervened in our lives, our story would have been much different. Our only cloud on that day was that Ray's family was not there to witness our 'sending out'. Ray's Mum and Dad were on holiday. It truly was hard for Ray to obey God, but as he trusted Him, Ray's relationship with his Mum and Dad actually got stronger and they have been very faithful in supporting us throughout the years.

On 1st June 1980, we left the security of our lovely home in Scotland and moved to England to join British Youth for Christ. We rented our three-bedroom bungalow out to some friends who said they would keep our bedroom for us whenever we came back. (Ray had told his parents that he would come back every month for a further year to work in the shop for one week to help them out.) We had to leave our fantastic sporty car because it belonged to the business and so as we left by train that day, we were excited at all that lay ahead, but also a little apprehensive.

We were so pleased that our friends Rob and Liz Marshall had asked us to come and stay with them. The house they were renting belonged to British Youth for Christ but they gladly opened their home to us. I have to say that although it was wonderful to stay with them, the whole move to Wolverhampton was such a culture shock to us. The house was situated in the red-light district of Wolverhampton and the prostitutes gathered outside the front window as they looked for business. We had come from a middle-class district and here we were in one of the poorest areas of Wolverhampton. The house had damp running down its walls; in fact Rob and Liz could not use the front room of the house because the damp was so bad. While we had been used to a middle-class existence I have to say that, despite the culture shock, we were extremely happy. We knew we were doing what God had called us to do and being with our good friends, Rob and Liz, gave us the extra security we needed through our initial months in BYFC.

When we walked through the door of the Youth for Christ offices on our first day, we received another surprise. There was a small group of office staff sitting in a circle. As they looked up to see who was coming through the door and before anyone even said 'hello', we were told in no uncertain terms by one of the administrators that we were late. We had been told by Clive Calver to be there for 9.00 am but realised after we arrived that they had a prayer meeting at 8.45 am. When we asked where we were to work from, we were told we could have a corner of someone's desk. The person who was in charge of the offices was ill at the time and if he had been there, our welcome to British Youth for Christ would have been much different. It was not the best start to full-time Christian work. However, the joy and fulfilment in our hearts at being in the centre of God's will overcame whatever problems and difficulties we encountered. We knew this was where God wanted us to be. It really doesn't matter where you are, as long as you know you are doing what God wants you to do. The best place to find fulfilment is in the centre of God's will for your life. Ray and I knew we had done what God had called us to do and we were only at the beginning of a great adventure of faith.

Our first nine months in BYFC were very difficult and I'm sure if God had not called us so clearly we would have been tempted to give up and go home. We had come with a vision of starting a team/band that would show young people what Jesus was really like. While we prayed and asked God to fulfil our dreams, we were asked to head up the creative arts section, which meant working with musicians such as Graham Kendrick and my close friend, Sheila Walsh. Although we had some fantastic times working with Graham and Sheila, those nine months were the worst nine months of our lives. We really did not enjoy what we were doing in the office section of our job and yet God taught us and shaped us so much through that time. We learned so much through Clive Calver, Ken McGreavy and many other great leaders in BYFC. We are so grateful for the love they showed and the investment they made into our lives.

Right at the time when we were at our lowest, we were offered a job by another Christian organisation. It sounded so tempting when they explained that we would head up a team in their organisation and not only get a bigger salary but we would also have paid holidays abroad each year. We were very flattered to be asked, but as we talked through the possibilities and prayed about it, deep down we knew we were to stay where we were at present. I remember on several occasions, when tensions were high, having to stop Ray from lifting the phone and telling the other organisation we would join them. Even though we were going through some difficult times, God knew what He was doing. It was hard but we learned so much through our first nine months that was to help us enormously in our leadership skills at a later stage.

It was also during those nine months that we carried and birthed our dream of having a team who were musicians but who were sold-out to God. As we prayed, without advertising, God brought to us four people who were to join us in the band we called Heartbeat. A few months before starting Heartbeat, we shared our vision with a wise and godly couple, Alex and Peggy Buchanan. As we spoke with them and they prayed for us, they warned us not to think about starting a band/team such as Heartbeat unless we were going to make prayer a priority. They stressed how important it was to seek God's face and hear His voice. As we left them with their words ringing in our ears, we determined to make prayer a priority not only in our lives but also in the life of the team. As we travelled around the country with a vision to be a demonstration of God's power and love, we did not realise the enormity of what God would accomplish through us. We were right at the beginning of an amazing story of God's faithfulness and although we didn't realise it we were in a 'school of learning', discovering what it meant to 'live by faith' in every area of our lives.

Exercises for your faith muscles

Think through/discuss the following questions:

► Is prayer a priority in your life? Write down ways of making it more of a priority in your life. No one finds prayer easy. Discuss or think through the problems you face when you pray and how you can overcome them.

► Is God calling you to step out in a new direction? Take time to lay down your life before Him and ask Him to have full control. Ask God to confirm His agenda for your life.

► John 14:1 says *'Trust in God, trust also in me.'* Write down/discuss times in the past when you have trusted in God. What did you learn from that experience? Then write down/discuss a time when you did not trust in God. What did you learn from that experience?

► Meditate on Psalm 37:3–4. Write down/discuss what you receive from God.

► Memorise 2 Corinthians 5:7:

   'We live by faith and not by sight.'

Chapter 3

Sacrifice of Faith

'Just let me get this right – you are saying that God wants us to sacrifice our offices and give them away?'

After we had been in British Youth for Christ for just under three years, Ray and I began to feel God was asking us to leave BYFC and set up Heartbeat as a separate ministry. As we prayed and sought God, we felt that God was asking us to 'live by faith' and depend on Him for our finances. This was indeed a very scary thought. In BYFC, we had a salary each of £2,500 per year and although it was small at least it was regular. As we prayed about this we decided to share our thoughts with the rest of Heartbeat. I remember vividly sitting with the team whilst Ray and I explained what we felt God had been saying to us. We were careful to say that God *might* only be saying to the two of us that we should 'live by faith for our finances'. However, we asked them to go and pray and see if they felt this was something from God for us all. As we finished sharing what God had laid on our hearts, our keyboard player, Dave Bankhead exclaimed, 'Well . . . I think I need a stiff drink!' He may have only been joking, but his comments did bring home to us the reality of what God might be asking us to do.

After a week of praying on our own the six of us sat down together to discuss what each individual felt God had said. We had an amazing team of people; each one of them very special people who we knew would really seek God's heart for the way forward. We were amazed and thrilled when every one of them told us that they were in this move with us. Each one felt that they should move out of BYFC and begin to live by faith. As we sat and discussed the future, we knew we were on the edge of an exciting journey of faith yet I am sure if we had been honest, each one of us would have said that we were apprehensive and scared about the way ahead. We had no idea about what we would encounter, but we did know that God was walking with us and that gave us confidence to take the first step.

Ray and I went to share our thoughts and the scriptures God had given us with the leadership of BYFC. We had valued our time in that organisation and we were so thankful for all they had done to help us in our early years as Heartbeat. The leadership understood totally what we were saying and released us in August 1983 from the salaried staff of BYFC. We left not having any PA equipment, no lights, van, offices or money! All we had was our personal gear: our drums, keyboard, guitars etc., and the promise that God would supply *all* our needs.

As you can imagine we spent quite a lot of time together during our last few months in BYFC praying and seeking God as to where we should set up our base. We came into contact with a man and two girls who told us how they used to be an administration team for another ministry called Living Sound. A few months earlier they felt that God had told them to leave and that He would show them a team that they could serve in administration. As we prayed and talked together for some weeks, it became apparent that as well as their providing the secretarial and administrative support we needed, we should all move to Malmesbury, Wiltshire and set up our base there. The Shaftsbury Society had a school there for physically and mentally handicapped children and they had kindly offered us a wing of their building where we could set up our offices on a peppercorn rent. We were so excited. God provided not only administration help for us (up until then I had been doing all the administration on the road) but had also given us four offices and a lounge with kitchen combined.

In August 1983 we all began to move our homes to a very beautiful part of the country that we did not know even existed before we heard the word 'Malmesbury'. We were to live and have our offices there for the next ten years. About a year later, however, we were to go through one of the biggest lessons of faith that we could learn.

The man who had become our administrator had decided he wanted to leave Heartbeat, and as he had found the offices in the first place he wanted Ray and me and the rest of the team to leave so he could use them for his new ministry. As you can imagine we were shocked as we felt the offices were not his but ours. However, as usual we all went to God in prayer over the issue and also phoned our faithful and wise pastor and friend, Ken McGreavy. When Ray and I had started Heartbeat in 1981, we had approached Ken McGreavy who was not only a good friend of ours but who was also the pastor of British Youth for Christ at the time. We had asked him if he would mentor Ray and me and stand with us as we pursued God's vision for our lives. Ken had said he would, and he and Hazel, his wife, have been so faithful to us over the years. They pray for us both every day and have given us mountains of wisdom and advice over the years as well as becoming two of our trustees when we became a registered charity in 1985.

Ray and I arranged to meet Ken at a service station on the M4. When we discussed with Ken what was happening with our offices, we were shocked to hear that he felt that we needed to do an 'Abraham' and put our offices on the altar. We could not believe that Ken was telling us that we should 'sacrifice' our offices and give them to our administrator. Ray and I looked at each other, surely that could not be what God was asking us to do? The more we talked and prayed with Ken, the more it became obvious that this was indeed the right course of action.

As we drove back to Malmesbury in the car, we began to wonder how the team would receive the news that we no longer had a set of offices. We needn't have worried though because after the initial shock, they began to see that no matter what, God would provide for us. We called our administrator and told him that he could have the offices and began to make plans to set up our administration base in our home. We also informed the school that we would be moving out of the building. It 'just so happened' that the head of the Shaftesbury Society at that time, Gordon Holloway, was coming to visit the school at Malmesbury and asked if he could see Ray. When Ray met him in the Headmaster's office, the first thing Gordon said was, 'I only need to know the answer to one question. Do you want to leave the offices?' When Ray said 'No', he immediately responded and said, 'The offices are yours. We never gave the offices in the first place to your administrator: we gave them to Heartbeat and we still believe God wants you to have them. I will chat with the person concerned and will let him know that the offices belong to you.' We could not believe what God had done. We thought our offices were dead but here was God raising them back to life again. As we had been obedient to what God had said, God had performed a miracle.

Thousands of years previously, when Abraham went up the mountain to sacrifice his son, he knew that he would put the knife in his precious son's body. He did not know what God would do; he only knew that he must be obedient and trust that somehow God would raise Isaac back to life. God wanted to find out whether Abraham would be obedient to Him. When God saw Abraham's heart, He stopped him from harming his son and provided a ram as a sacrifice instead (Genesis 22). When situations and decisions seem incredibly tough, it is good to listen and read about how God has dealt with others in a similar situation. Ken had indeed heard the word of the Lord to us. Never in our wildest dreams did we think that God would give us back our offices. We knew God would somehow provide for us, but we were prepared to set up an office in our home and work from there. As we 'killed' our offices off, God raised them back to life for us. As you can imagine, we were ecstatic and so grateful to God and to the Shaftesbury Society for what they had given us.

Exercises for your faith muscles

Read Genesis 22:1–18, the story of how Abraham was asked to sacrifice Isaac.

► How would you feel if God asked you to 'sacrifice' something or someone very special to you? Write down/discuss your response.

► Abraham must have found obedience to God in these circumstances very difficult. He had no way of knowing that God would step in before he plunged the knife into his precious son. He exercised his faith and trusted that God had the power to raise the dead (Hebrews 11:19). How easy/hard do you find obedience to God in your life and why? Take a look at 1 Samuel 15 for further study on obedience.

► God was pleased with Abraham's obedience and response. What did God say and promise to Abraham? See Genesis 22:15–18. What does God promise us when we obey Him? See Mark 10:29–30.

► Memorise 1 Samuel 15:22:

   'To obey is better than sacrifice.'

Chapter 4

Growing in Faith

'Ray, Nancy, I am sorry to have to tell you that the church has decided tonight that your financial support has stopped.'

Ray and I could not believe what we were hearing. A few months after we had come off salary with British Youth for Christ, Ray's father phoned us to say that they had just attended a church meeting where it had been decided that the church would no longer financially support Ray and myself in the work we were doing. I could tell that Ray's parents were very upset at this decision and felt that they should warn us that the cheque we were expecting in the next couple of weeks would not arrive. What Ray's parents did not know, however, was that a week or so earlier, Ray and I had felt challenged from God to give away everything we received as our regular income for that month. We regularly received three gifts, one large gift of £400 from our church and two smaller ones of £30 each from two friends. This was not enough for us to live on so we always had to reach out to God each month to receive the extra we needed. A great need for money to support evangelism had arisen and as we had prayed about it we had felt challenged by God to give away everything we received regularly and depend on Him for all our needs for that month. Although we regularly gave to God's work, this was the first time that God had ever asked us to give away a full month's 'salary'. As we gave it, I can remember thinking to myself that we only needed to get through the next few weeks and then the church money would come in again. Now here was Ray's dad telling us that the church money would not be arriving.

To say that we were shocked was an understatement. We could not believe it. Perhaps Ray's dad had got it wrong? However, when no letter or cheque arrived over the next three months we realised that he had heard correctly. On the night we heard the news fear crept into our hearts. We talked long into the night discussing what God was doing. Did He want us to give up our work in evangelism with Heartbeat? Did He want us to go and get jobs? We talked, prayed and cried together and resolved that in the morning we needed to phone and talk with our friends, Ken and Hazel McGreavy. We knew they would pray with us and together we would discover what God was saying. After hours of talking, Ray went into the kitchen to get a drink and discovered that the old dishwasher we had brought with us a few years before when we left Scotland, was on fire. This was the last straw – what else could go wrong?

The next morning we phoned our friends and told them our sorry tale. Ken immediately invited us to travel down to their home in London to see them. As we got into our car at Preston, we put on a teaching cassette by Floyd McClung and as we listened, we realised that God was speaking to us. Floyd said, 'At times you may feel you are out on a limb for God and when you look back it's as if you see the devil sawing off the branch.' This was exactly what Ray and I had felt. We had given everything we had to live on. We had no savings to fall back on. We needed God to somehow do something in order for us to survive. We had a mortgage to pay and we needed food to eat, but as we looked for God to provide, it was as if we saw the enemy sawing off our branch. Were we going to fall big-time?

Floyd went on to say 'I tell you even though you see the devil sawing off the branch, God will enable the branch to stay in the air and the tree will fall down.' Right at that moment, God spoke to us and said, 'Ray, Nancy, what have you been praying for?' We suddenly remembered that we had been praying for God to increase our faith. We felt the Lord say, 'I am just answering your prayers.' What a relief to know that God was still with us and that all He wanted us to do was to trust Him. As I mentioned in the introductory chapter, there are three steps to discovering real faith pumping through our veins. The first is hearing from God; the second is obedience to what God is saying and the third is trusting God and His Word. We had heard God tell us to give away our regular income; we had been obedient and had released the finance. Now we needed to take the third step of trusting God despite the circumstances. As we travelled in the car we prayed and thanked God for what He was doing with us and asked Him to help us to trust Him and to therefore grow in our faith. As we finished praying we realised that our joy had returned and our heavy hearts had disappeared. God was with us and if God was with us then He would somehow provide. It may have looked as though we had nothing but in actual fact we had everything because we had God! When we arrived at Ken and Hazel's home in London we were delighted to tell them that God had already spoken to us.

During the next few months, God did some pretty amazing things. The branch certainly did stay in the air. We had been trying to sell our home for months with no success, but that month our house sold, which freed us to move from Preston in Lancashire to Malmesbury in Wiltshire where God had given us a base from which to work. When we arrived in Malmesbury, Ray and I put our bed in one of the offices and shared the kitchen with the rest of Heartbeat during the day. A few weeks later God provided a huge home rent-free for three months. The local vicarage was empty as the local Church of England was waiting for a new vicar to arrive. They very kindly told us that we and another couple in Heartbeat who were looking for a home could stay in the vicarage for the summer until the vicar arrived. Our income was greatly reduced, however God reduced our outgoings even more for a period of time.

Our church in Scotland had been going through some really tough issues at the time and all the elders and some of the deacons who had commissioned us and sent us out as missionaries had left to start up another church nearby called Kyle Community Church. When they heard that the church they had left had stopped supporting us, they immediately decided to take up an offering for us each month. Twenty-one years later, they are still supporting us as their missionaries. Their constant financial and prayerful support has been an amazing blessing to us both as a couple and now to us as a family. They have been extremely loving, caring and generous. They have never put demands on us but continue to faithfully pray for us. We know that because of their generosity and care they will receive a rich blessing when they arrive in heaven. It is so encouraging to work with them and have them partner with us in seeing people's lives changed.

This experience taught us how to grow in faith. We honestly never thought that when we asked God to increase our faith we would go through such pressure, and yet we certainly learned loads about what it is really like to depend on God for our finances. There have been many similar journeys we have been on during our lives and each one has helped us to grow more in love with our Lord Jesus. I have often said throughout the twenty-four years that I have lived this way, that every Christian should 'live by faith for their finances' for at least a year of their lives. It certainly is the quickest way of getting to know the Lord and discovering that He is real and alive today.

One of the lessons we have learned along our journey of faith is that it is extremely important to honour God with our money. Tithing was never taught at my church in Scotland. I attended a Christian Brethren church for the first twenty-two years of my life where I was taught that giving ten per cent was part of the 'old' covenant and that really all your finances belonged to God. However, in reality, many people only ever gave the change in their pockets and even ten per cent was never reached.

When Ray and I married, the thought of giving ten per cent of our income to God was something that seemed immoral to us. Many years before God led us into full-time Christian work,

He taught us an important lesson about tithing. One Sunday evening, not long after we were married, we attended a church in Glasgow where an evangelist called Ian Leitch was speaking. During the service I strongly felt that God had told me to give Ian some money. This kind of thing had never happened to me before and so I thought I would chat it through with Ray whenever we got a chance to do so. After the meeting we were invited to someone's home for supper and discovered that the preacher, Ian, had been invited too. We really liked Ian and spent most of the night chatting with him. As we left to go, he delighted us by inviting us to spend a weekend with him and his wife at his home in a couple of months' time. We didn't realise it, but this was a friendship which was to last a huge number of years. We were to learn so much through Ian and Morag Leitch.

On the way home, Ray surprised me by telling me that during the service he had felt God say to him that we should be giving Ian a gift of money. We spent the rest of that evening discussing what we should do. How much should we send? Would Ian think it was weird if we sent him money through the post? We did not know if Ian was on a salary or how he got his money. As there were so many unanswered questions, we decided to think and pray about it individually and discuss it again in a couple of days.

When we brought the subject back up again in a couple of days, neither of us was any clearer about what we should do. It did seem strange to send someone we didn't really know some money through the post. Maybe he didn't need it; maybe we did not hear from God? So many doubts filled our minds that we delayed it for another few days. When we talked about it again at a later stage, we convinced ourselves that it was now too late to send any money and we somehow must have got it wrong. We had both heard God speak to us so clearly and yet we allowed our doubts and fears to distract us from what He had said. We ended up not doing what God had asked us to do. In the coming weeks we forgot all about it.

After a few months, it was time for us to drive to the east

coast of Scotland to where Ian and Morag lived. During that
weekend, we asked Ian about his financial base and discovered
that he 'lived by faith' and depended on God to send him
enough money to live on. Ray asked him if there had been any
time that God had let him down. Ian replied 'It's funny you
should ask that, because there was a time just recently, in fact it
was around the time that I met you where I was praying for
God to send me some money to cover a bill. My time limit
came and went and I couldn't understand why God had not
sent the money in on time. Eventually, however, God did send
the money through from a contact in the States.'

Ray and I looked at each other and then confessed to Ian that
we knew why God had not sent in the money at the correct
time. We had disobeyed God and had not done what God had
asked us to do. Ian then asked us a question that was to lay a
huge foundation in our lives for our future. He asked us if we
tithed our finances. We admitted we didn't and told him all
our excuses as to why we didn't. Ian went through the Bible
with us and showed us why it was essential that at least ten per
cent of our income should go to God. We remember quite
clearly telling Ian that if we gave ten per cent of our salary to
God we would be even more in the red each month. We
explained that we had very small salaries and at the end of each
month our bank account went into the red for a few days
before our salaries arrived. We told Ian in no uncertain terms
that we could not afford to tithe. Ian's reply stuck in our hearts
and minds as he said to us, 'You can't afford not to tithe. If you
trust God in this and do what He is telling you to do, instead of
being in the red each month you will be in the black.'

We arrived home knowing that we needed to take the step of
trusting God for our money. The very next month we tithed
our finances and gave ten per cent away. It felt good to be
doing what God had instructed us to do and at the end of that
month, for the first time ever in our married life, we were in the
black. It is so important to put God first and honour Him with
our finances. God says in Malachi 3:8–9 that if we do not tithe
and give offerings then it amounts to *robbing* God. But when

we do tithe, God says He will *'throw open the floodgates of heaven and pour out so much blessing that you will not have room enough for it'* (Malachi 3:10).

In Matthew 23:23 Jesus makes it clear that we should not forget to tithe. Why is it that we struggle so much to give back to God just a little of what He has given us? Jesus quite clearly says,

'You cannot serve both God and Money.'   (Matthew 6:24)

Money can have such a hold on our lives as I discovered a few months later.

My husband, Ray, is one of the most generous people I have ever met. He would give away his last penny to someone who needed it more than he did. When he came to me a few months after we had begun to tithe and told me that he wanted to give away the only savings we had, I was indignant. It is one thing to give God the first ten per cent, but surely God would not ask me to part with our savings account. We had £200 in an account put aside for something special like a holiday and here was Ray saying that he wanted to pray and ask God if we should give it away to someone else. That night in bed I could not sleep; instead I argued with God. I was determined that God was not going to get His hands on that money. That money was mine and I wanted to spend it on something that would be special for Ray and me. I argued back and forth with God for what seemed like hours and then I hit the bed with my clenched fist and shouted out loud, *'No!'* The act of shouting at God suddenly brought me to my senses. I could not believe what I had done. I loved the Lord so much and yet here I was shouting 'No' at Him. I very quickly repented and told God I was sorry. I told Him that if He wanted my savings He could have them, in fact He could have every penny I owned. As I poured out my heart to God, a huge relief flooded my being and to be honest I could not believe it had taken me so long to say 'Yes' and give in to God.

One of the biggest hindrances to our faith is not honouring

God with our finances. Without necessarily realising it, we can get very 'precious' about *our* money. God broke something in me that night that changed my attitude to finance and helped me to realise that there is much joy in giving; in fact there can be more joy in giving than in receiving. Not only that, but God loves a cheerful giver (2 Corinthians 9:7).

Throughout the years God showed me that if I obeyed Him and gave out of the little I had, He would provide abundantly for me. I know from experience that it is true that you can never out-give God. No matter how big our shovel is, God's shovel is always bigger. As we shovel our tithes and offerings out with our little shovel, God will use His massive shovel to pour His blessings into our lives.

God knew all those years ago that if we did not get these principles right in our lives, then it would be impossible for us to live by faith and depend on Him for the finances we needed not only to survive but also to succeed. Can I encourage you to put your finances under the Lordship of Christ? All our money and possessions belong to Him anyhow, we are just caretakers of it. Let's make sure that we look after His money the way He would want us to. We must not hold it to ourselves, but surrender our will to His and do what He tells us to do with the wealth He has given us. We tell the young missionaries who join ngm each year that they cannot expect God to answer their prayers for finance if they are not honouring Him in the first place with their personal finances. It's not a matter of how much money we have; it is a matter of allowing God to have full access to all that we have and being open to when, how and to whom he may want us to give. As we were told many years ago, you cannot afford not to tithe.

Exercises for your faith muscles

Read Malachi 3:8–12.

► Take a good look at your personal finances. Are you honouring God with your money? Pray and ask God if there are any changes you should make. Write down what God says to you and then tick them off when you have put them into practice. Take time to ask God if there are any missionaries you should be supporting.

▶ Meditate on Ecclesiastes 5:10: *'Whoever loves money never has money enough; whoever loves wealth is never satisfied with his income.'* Write down/discuss what God says.

▶ Read 1 Kings 17:7–16. Write down/discuss what God says to you through this portion of scripture.

▶ Memorise Proverbs 3:9–10:

> *'Honour the LORD with your wealth,*
> * with the firstfruits of all your crops;*
> *then your barns will be filled to overflowing,*
> * and your vats will brim over with new wine.'*

Chapter 5

Faith for the Impossible

'That van will not get us to the end of the street, never mind the other end of the country!'

Just after we had left Youth for Christ, and had set up our own ministry under the name of Heartbeat, the need for a van became evident. In British Youth for Christ we had used a van, which we had called the Bread Bin, as it seemed to want to cook you red hot. We hadn't liked the van very much, but in comparison to the van we had just borrowed, our van in BYFC began to look like the best thing since sliced bread! Ray took one look at the van we had borrowed which was supposed to take us on a five-hour journey to Lowestoft at the end of the week and said 'This is ridiculous! This van will not get us to the end of the street, never mind the other end of the country.' Ray immediately encouraged us to go to God in prayer, as he felt God had a better and more suitable van for us.

We called the whole of Heartbeat together, and as we prayed and asked God for a van we heard Him speak clearly to us. God simply asked us, 'What kind of van do you want? Be specific!' We discussed the kind of van we would need and came up with a complete profile of the van. We felt that a Mercedes would be the best make, possibly a 307D. It had to be a certain height; depth and length because of our equipment, but it didn't need to be brand new. It could be around two or three years old and we reckoned it would possibly cost us between £5,000 and £6,000. We wrote all the information down and even had a photograph of the van we wanted. We put the information and the photo in the middle of the floor and again prayed to God.

As we prayed and told God this was the kind of van we wanted, we felt we should contact a friend of a friend who dealt in Mercedes vans. During the phone call, the guy informed us that these vans were really scarce as most people held on to them for a long time, however he needed to know our time scale. When did we need the van? He almost collapsed when we told him that we needed the van by Saturday, as this was when we were going off on our mission to Lowestoft. He told us he would phone us back as soon as he had made some enquiries, but as we put the phone down his last words were ringing in our ears: 'It will take a miracle to get this type of van by Saturday!' We laughed and said, 'He doesn't realise it, but that is exactly what we are needing!'

During our band rehearsals the next day, which was Thursday, we received a phone call from our garage friend who told us excitedly, 'You will never believe this! I have found the exact van you wanted. It's a 307D with the exact dimensions you asked for. It is two years old and will cost you £5,400.' You can imagine the excitement we had in our hearts as we sent someone off to look at the van. There was only one little problem! We didn't have the money; in fact we didn't have a penny towards this van. We prayed again asking God to complete the miracle by giving us enough finance so that we could purchase this vehicle. We then went back downstairs to rehearse. Ten minutes later we had a phone call from someone Ray and I did not know but who lived in our local town of Malmesbury. During his prayer time that morning with his wife, this man had heard God clearly speak to him and say 'I want you to phone the offices of Heartbeat and offer them an amount of money they need to purchase a van.' We had our van and we went off to our mission in Lowestoft with our miracle and a new story of God's amazing faithfulness.

One of the important lessons we learned through that

journey of faith was the need to be specific in our prayers. Often our prayers can be vague. We ask God to bless us but we are not specific about exactly what we would like God to do. This is one of the hindrances to seeing our faith grow. God taught us through this journey that it was important to be specific in our prayers. We read in Mark 10 that when Jesus asked Bartimaeus what he wanted, Bartimaeus didn't say, 'Oh I'm not really sure what I want you to do!' No, he was specific and immediately replied to Jesus with the words, *'I want to see'* (Mark 10:51). It was obvious to everyone that Bartimaeus was blind but to unlock the miracle of receiving his eyesight required him to be specific.

Similarly if God were to ask you today, 'What do you want Me to do for you?' I wonder how many of us would be specific with God. Would we have to stop and think what we would like to receive from God or would our response be immediate? Bartimaeus' need was such that he knew immediately what his priority was in prayer. What is your priority in prayer today? Be specific and don't be afraid to ask God for a miracle. After all, all miracles have their origin in our Father God.

Many years later, when Ray and I were asking God for a holiday, we put this principle into action again. After we had been praying together for some time about a holiday for our son, Daniel, and ourselves, I turned to Ray and asked him, 'Where would you like to go on holiday?' His answer surprised me. I thought he would say somewhere abroad, but he said 'I'd really like to go to the Lake District.' We then began to pray specifically for a holiday in the Lake District, which is situated in a very beautiful part of England.

A few days later we received a phone call from a very good friend of ours who said he and his wife would like to take us on holiday with them. We thought this would be our answer to prayer, however when we compared dates we realised that we couldn't make the dates that they were offering. He then said he would look at the dates again and get back to us. Five days later his daughter phoned to say, 'It's all booked up.' I was amazed and answered, 'I don't understand. What do you mean it's all booked up? I thought you couldn't make our dates.' She told me that her Mum and Dad had booked us all into a hotel and that they would stay for the weekend and we would stay for the week. I could not believe her reply when I asked her where they had booked. They had booked us into a luxurious hotel in the Lake District. They had no idea that we were praying for a holiday in the Lake District. We had been specific and God had opened up the way for a wonderful fun-filled holiday for Ray, Daniel and myself. God is so good ... and our friends are pretty amazing too.

Exercises for your faith muscles

Read Mark 10:46–52, 1 Kings 3:5–15 and 2 Kings 2:1–14.

► In each of these portions of scripture the question is asked, 'What do you want me to do for you?' Each person immediately responds with a specific answer. Write down/ discuss what you can learn from this on being specific in your own relationship with the Lord.

► Write down/discuss any reasons that would hinder you from being specific. Bring each one before the Lord.

► God's blessings were bestowed upon the three persons mentioned in the above portions of scripture. Spend some time praying for a specific need and write down what God says to you. If He gives you any instructions then do make sure you are obedient to what He says.

► Memorise Hebrews 10:23:

> 'Let us hold unswervingly to the hope we profess, for he who promised is faithful.'

Chapter 6

Faith for Healing

'My arm! My arm!' shouted one teenager as our concert was coming to a close. Malcolm Morgan, one of our youth workers, went to speak with him and discovered an amazing story of God's power in action.

Early in the '80s when we were finishing one of our missions, we saw God move in healing for the first time. We had been singing and speaking in the schools of the local area and at the end of the week, we invited the school pupils to come and see us play at a local hall. After we had spoken and sung and Ray had preached, Ray invited people to stand up if they wanted to come to know the Lord. Many responded, but as one young teenager stood, he suddenly shouted out, 'My arm! My arm!' We discovered after Malcolm had spoken to him that he had come into the event with his arm in a sling. His wrist had been broken and after six weeks he had gone to the hospital to get the plaster removed, but they had discovered that the bone had been set wrongly and therefore he would have to go back into hospital and get his bone set correctly. As the boy stood to say he wanted to ask God into his life, he felt a heat go through his arm and he was instantaneously healed. Neither Ray nor myself nor any of Heartbeat was expecting God to heal that night, but God did it anyhow. We were astonished and so were the boy's friends, who all came to know the Lord too because they had seen God's power in action.

Some time after that, Ray and I attended a conference for leaders on the subject of healing, which was hosted and organised by Ken McGreavy. The evangelist who had been asked to speak at this event was Ian Andrews. Ian has seen God use him in incredible ways as he speaks throughout the world. He talked about how the Lord had commissioned us to preach the Gospel *and* heal the sick (Luke 9:2) and how if we were evangelists then we needed to take up the challenge of preaching the gospel and healing the sick. We left the conference feeling that God had placed 'a seed of faith' in our hearts that when we preached the gospel at any of our Heartbeat missions, some people would get healed as a sign that God was real.

Our first mission after this conference was in Bristol. I remember us all praying like crazy before the event that God would move in salvation *and* healing. We were very nervous as Ray got up to speak that night but we were thrilled to see that at the appeal many gave their lives to Christ. Ray then took a deep breath and in fear and trembling said, 'Now I believe that some of you are going to be healed.' As Ray prayed and released the Holy Spirit to bring healing, the rest of us were all praying, 'God, just one! Just heal one person Lord!' Our faith was small but we took up the challenge, obeyed, and put our trust in God. That night we were amazed, relieved and excited to discover that eleven people were healed of various diseases. God is fantastic! Ray and I cannot heal anyone, but over the years since that time we have literally seen God heal hundreds of people.

I remember a girl in Northern Ireland being healed of a back complaint. She was listening to Ray preaching during a Heartbeat concert and as she watched she saw a vision of Jesus standing behind Ray. Jesus looked at her and pointed to her and in that instance she was healed of a back complaint she had had for years.

Another young teenage boy told us that he had been healed of a hole in his heart. We had encouraged him to go to his doctor and get checked out medically before coming off any medication the doctor had given him. When we visited Northern Ireland a year later, he came to see us to tell us that he had been back to his doctor and after an examination and X-rays, the doctor had said he did not understand it but there was no hole in his heart now.

At one of our missions in England, we prayed for a teenage girl who had a cartilage problem in her knee. We knew medically she could not be healed of this but needed God to do a complete miracle by providing her with a new cartilage. She felt the heat of the Holy Spirit go through her knee as we prayed and immediately knew that she had been healed. She went back into school on the Monday and asked her head teacher if she could now take PE lessons as God had healed her knee. Her head teacher wisely told her she needed to go to the doctor and get a letter from him confirming that she could now restart taking PE lessons. She went to the doctor and told him that God had healed her. He was not convinced until he examined her knee and proclaimed that he did not know what had happened and that although it was medically impossible, she was indeed healed. He gave her the letter she wanted and she was able to start PE lessons again. Isn't our God incredible?

After one of our events in Redhill, a man wrote to us and told us that in January he had had heart problems and that after tests his doctor had told him that he had had a mild heart attack and he was promptly put on medication. In June, during our worship event, he had felt the power of God go through him and he knew he had been healed. The pain went instantly and his heart started beating properly. When he went back to the doctor, he was put through an ECG which showed no signs of him ever having had a heart attack. What a fantastic God we serve!

At one of our events in Preston a man with a massive hernia suddenly shouted 'It's gone!' His massive hernia had disappeared. Another teenage lad came to one of our camps with eczema. As he was prayed for, you could visibly see God healing him. Dry flaky skin started to fall from his body as he stood at the front of the meeting. New fresh clean skin appeared all over his body and he told us that this was the first time in fifteen years that he had felt soft skin. At the same meeting, during one of our worship times, a young teenage lad suddenly shouted out *'Brilliant!'* Ian Townend, our guitarist, went over to him to find him reading his Bible with his left eye shut! He told Ian he had a weak right eye and could not see close up. During the worship time, God had touched him and his eye was instantly healed.

I am praying that these stories will inspire you not only to believe for healing in your own life, but also to take up the challenge to pray for healing for your friends. When people who don't know God see God move in healing power, it makes them realise that God is indeed alive.

Often people think that it is only special people who have a healing ministry who can pray for someone and see them healed, but that is not the case. God will use anyone who has a small grain of faith. A few years ago, when my son Aidan was only three or four years of age, I discovered that he had prayed for someone and had seen her healed. Aidan knows that when we are ill we always pray and ask God to make us better. One day whilst having his lunch in the ngm offices, he overheard his favourite cousin, Natalie, mention that she had a huge headache that she could not shift. Without prompting from anyone, Aidan got up from his seat and went over to Natalie, laid his hand on her head and said, 'Lord Jesus, please make Natalie better, Amen.' A simple prayer combined with a simple faith. Instantaneously, Natalie was amazed to discover that she was healed. God will use the simplest of prayers and the smallest amount of faith to perform a miracle.

I don't know everything there is to know about healing, but what I do know is that when we demonstrate the smallest portion of *real* faith in God, miracles happen. Jesus tells us,

> ' ... *if you have faith as small as a mustard seed, you can say to this mountain, "Move from here to there" and it will move. Nothing will be impossible for you.'* (Matthew 17:20)

It is important to remember, however, that faith has its origins in God. There is nothing we can do to work faith up. We cannot manufacture it, but we can ask God to increase our faith.

As I said earlier, neither Ray nor I can heal anyone, only God can heal. There have been times when we have prayed for individuals and they haven't been healed. Sometimes there is a clear answer as to why the person hasn't been healed at that time; sometimes there is no answer. But one thing I do know is that God is a loving God who loves us all and wants us to be well. It is interesting to note that when Jesus was here on this earth not everyone that Jesus saw was healed. Only one of the people around the pool of Bethesda received healing from Jesus; however, everyone who came to Jesus for healing was healed.

The Lord always answers when real faith is present. It does not seem to matter who has that faith. It can be found in you or in the person you are praying for but it is important that faith is present. We find that when we pray in evangelistic situations for people to get healed, God seems to heal many as a sign and a wonder. However, when we pray at Christian celebrations there are not so many healed. I believe that lack of faith in this situation is the reason for this. The Bible tells us that faith is a gift of the Spirit (1 Corinthians 12:9) and a fruit of the Spirit (Galatians 5:22), but in either case faith comes from God. Can I encourage you to ask God to give you His faith to believe Him for more?

God plants faith in our hearts, but in order for it to grow we must use it. Faith only grows through us exercising it. We all know that if we don't exercise our bodies then our muscles become flabby, similarly if we don't exercise our faith our spiritual muscles will become flabby and then we will not understand why God is not answering our prayers. Exercise faith in God today and see Him do a miracle through you.

Exercises for your faith muscles

▶ Read Luke 8:41–56, 17:12–19 and John 5:1–15. Each person was healed in a different way. What can we learn about faith through this?

▶ Discuss/think through ways in which our faith can increase.

▶ Pray and ask God for opportunities to be able to offer to pray for your friends when they are ill. Remember then to look for the opportunities God gives you.

▶ Memorise 1 Thessalonians 5:24:

> *'The one who calls you is faithful and he will do it.'*

Chapter 7

Creative Faith

'I will give you 100% mortgage because I believe in your employer more than I believe in my normal clients' employers.'

We met Ian and Dorry Townend in March 1983 when we were looking for a guitarist to join our band, Heartbeat. When we first met them, we had no idea that these two people were to become two of our closest friends and that our friendship would last a lifetime. Ian is Scottish by birth but through joining a band called Living Sound, he met and married his American wife, Dorry. A year after they were married they felt the call of God to come to Britain. They did not know where God was calling them to, but they knew that like Abraham, they had to obey God and leave their home, friends and country and travel to England. Just as they were praying about this, a friend from England called them and asked if they were feeling a call to come and serve God in England. When they explained that they had indeed been praying about this, he explained that he felt God was asking them not only to hear the call but to obey by packing their bags and travelling to England. He explained that if they did that and trusted God, then He would open doors before them. This was the encouragement they needed and so with their church's blessing, they left; putting themselves fully into the hands of God.

When they arrived on British soil, they were told about a couple called Ray and Nancy Goudie, who were in a full-time Christian band and who were looking for a guitarist. Ian was a guitarist and singer and Dorry was a singer. Within a week, Ian was in Heartbeat and was playing at Spring Harvest (a national Christian camp) with us. Within a month or so, Dorry became one of our singers. They did not realise it at the time, but they were to be in Heartbeat for the next eight years and as they would say now, 'We were at the beginning of one of the greatest adventures in God that we have ever known.'

When they arrived in Malmesbury, they had hardly any financial support and no home to live in. Similar to us, they lived in our offices for some time before exploring how they could get a home of their own. In the natural realm it seemed like crazy to be thinking of renting or buying because they were living on $75 per month support from their church. The Lord spoke to Ian and Dorry through the parable of the talents in the Bible – they felt that for them, if they rented, it would be like taking God's money and hiding it in the ground. They knew they should buy a home even although there seemed no reasonable way of doing so. Some months previously God had given Ray a verse of scripture, which we believed was a promise from God to all of us in ngm. The verse came from Hosea:

> ' "I will settle them in their homes,"
> *declares the* LORD.'   (Hosea 11:11)

We knew that God would somehow give each of us a home as we put our faith in Him.

As a team we went to spend some time at Colin Urquhart's base called 'The Hyde'. Colin's book *Faith for the Future* had been a huge encouragement to Ray and myself as we had been going through similar experiences of living by faith. We felt it would be good to spend some time together as a team in a faith-filled atmosphere, so we went on a retreat there. At the same retreat was a man who was a building society manager and out of the blue he told us that if we ever needed a mortgage we should get in touch with him. When we explained that we didn't have a regular salary as such, he told us this was not a problem, as he believed in our employer more than he believed in some of his regular client's employers.

When Ian and Dorry found a house they wanted to buy, they knew it was going to take a miracle to enable them to purchase it as they had no money to put down as a deposit. As Ian, Dorry, Ray and I prayed we felt it was right to approach our friend, the building society manager, for a loan. When we did he gave them a 100% mortgage on the house. Ian and Dorry did not need a deposit and by the time their loan came through, God not only increased their regular monthly support but each month gave them enough money to cover the mortgage payments. When Ian and Dorry left ngm many years later they sold their home for more than twice the amount they had paid for it.

Years later we are still reminding God of His promise to provide homes for us all. In 1993, three of our administration staff were looking for a home to rent in Thornbury just after we had moved to the area. When we prayed for them one night at our ngm meeting, Ray felt we should pray and 'call into being those things that as yet do not exist' (see Romans 4:17). Within days, a couple of wonderful apartments came up for rent. Up until this time the landlady had never rented these apartments out, but she felt the time was right to do so. We knew God had answered our prayers and had called what did not exist into being. Ngm staff have been in those apartments ever since.

Just because something does not exist does not mean that God cannot call it into being. While Abraham had waited for many years for God to fulfil His promise of a son, he did not weaken in his faith. Instead

> ' . . . *he faced the fact that his body was as good as dead . . . and that Sarah's womb was also dead. Yet he did not waver through unbelief . . .* [Instead he] *was strengthened in his faith and gave glory to God, being fully persuaded that God had power to do what he had promised.'* (Romans 4:19–21)

There is a huge difference between hoping that God will do something, and knowing that God has said that it will happen. One is hope-against-hope that it will happen, almost like crossing your fingers and trying to wish your promise into being. The other is real faith. When you demonstrate real faith, even to just the weight of a grain of mustard seed, it will accomplish much more than tons of hope-against-hope.

We cannot 'wish' or 'make' things that do not exist come into being; only God can do miracles. But God will respond to real faith. Jesus said quite clearly,

> *'If you believe, you will receive whatever you ask for in prayer.'*
> (Matthew 21:22)

Many of us believe that God can speak and bring about a miracle, but the belief that Jesus is speaking about here is believing and *knowing* that God will do a miracle. There is a massive difference. As I said earlier we cannot work faith up. The only way to receive faith is from the Lord Himself. Do remember that faith is a gift of the Spirit and also a fruit of the Spirit – and God gives both. Let's go to the *'author and perfecter of our faith'* (Hebrews 12:2) and make the disciples' prayer our prayer: 'Lord, increase our faith' (Luke 17:5). Let's ask God to give us His faith to see those things He has promised come into being. Let's also allow ourselves to grow in faith and as we see God fulfil one promise, let's build on that and believe God for more.

Phil Ball, our Assistant Director at ngm, had been praying for some time that God would give him a good reliable car. One day, while driving on the motorway, he saw the car that he thought would be perfect for him. He prayed a very simple prayer asking God to give him a Vauxhall Vectra estate, a five-door model with black roof rails, a little aerial and low mileage. He did not tell anyone what kind of car he wanted but each time he saw that make of car on the roads, he continued to say, 'That's the car I would like, Lord.'

About six months later, when he arrived at one of our ngm

centres, he was met by a friend who while out on a bike ride that morning had felt God say to him to stop at a garage and purchase a car for Phil. The car he bought was the exact car of Phil's dreams. It was a Vauxhall Vectra estate; five-door model with black roof rails; a little aerial and low mileage. Only God knew Phil's request, but that was more than enough to bring it into being.

When we apply faith to our prayers we will believe even when it doesn't look like the thing is going to happen. Real faith kept Noah building his boat, even when there was no sign of a flood happening. Real faith kept the children of Israel marching around Jericho even though the walls were huge and thick, thick enough to build houses in them. Real faith took Moses and the nation of Israel to the Red Sea trusting that somehow God would take them across. Real faith saved Daniel when he was thrown into a den full of ferocious and hungry lions. Real faith saved Esther from death when she approached the king about saving her nation without being summoned. We need real faith and we only get that by keeping close to God.

In Matthew 8:5–13 a centurion who approached Jesus for help displays real faith. Even Jesus said He had not found anyone in all Israel with such great faith (Matthew 8:10). The centurion asked Jesus to heal his servant who was paralysed and suffering terribly. Jesus responded by saying He would go and heal the servant, but the centurion would not let Him. The centurion answered Jesus by saying,

> 'Lord, I do not deserve to have you come under my roof. But just say the word, and my servant will be healed. For I myself am a man under authority, with soldiers under me. I tell this one, "Go," and he goes; and that one, "Come," and he comes. I say to my servant, "Do this," and he does it.'   (Matthew 8:8–9)

Jesus then told him,

> 'Go! It will be done just as you believed it would.'
>   (Matthew 8:13)

Another man in John 4:46–54 came and begged Jesus to come and heal his son who was close to death. Jesus told the man,

> *'You may go. Your son will live.'* (John 4:50)

When did this man put his faith into action? When he came to see Jesus? I believe his faith really started when he turned from Jesus and went back home. He came to Jesus expecting Jesus to come back with him and lay His hands on his son, but Jesus did not do that. Instead he said 'Go home. Your son will live.' He had heard Jesus speak; now he needed to obey and trust that Jesus would keep His promise. Each step away from Jesus was a step of true faith. There was no evidence that his son was healed. There was no telephone that he could use to check how his son was. He had to exercise faith to believe that when he reached his home many miles away in Capernaum, what Jesus had said would come true. As he demonstrated real faith, God healed his son.

Let's demonstrate real faith in God today and see His seed of faith growing in our hearts.

Exercises for your faith muscles

▶ What is faith? See Hebrews 11:1. Discuss or think through the difference between faith and hope.

▶ Three things are essential in order for us to develop faith in our hearts – hearing God, obeying God and trusting God. Discuss or think through ways in which you can develop all three ingredients in your walk with God.

▶ Spend some time asking God to increase your faith by developing your intimacy, obedience and trust in Him.

▶ Memorise Hebrews 11:1:

> *'Now faith is being sure of what we hope for and certain of what we do not see.'*

Chapter 8

Journey of Faith

'I want you to be a voice to the nation and not just a voice to the church.'

During 1984 Ray and I both felt we had heard God speak to us and say that one day He would take us to Johannesburg. When God first told us that He would take us to that city we did not even realise that it was in South Africa. However, from that time on we prayed that when the time was right to go we would know it. I remember responding to a call one day in a church in Stroud when the preacher asked people who felt they had been called to Africa to stand. Ray and I knew we had to stand and publicly tell people that we believed one day God would take us to South Africa.

About six months later it became obvious through our readings in the Bible and through God's whisper to our hearts that the time was right to go. In our travels we had met a Christian leader who when he heard that we were thinking of going to South Africa invited us to travel with him. It just so happened that he was going there on a speaking tour in April of that year. It was such a relief to be at least travelling with someone we knew, as we felt so 'alone' in our adventure of faith. We had never been to South Africa before and to travel into the unknown seemed so daunting. The Christian leader gave us the name and number of his co-ordinator and asked us to contact him to find out what flights he was on and see if we could co-ordinate our flights. We phoned his contact and discovered the cost of the flights and asked the rest of Heartbeat to pray for us. We did not know why God wanted us to go; just that we needed to be obedient and that He would show us why when we got there. We felt it was not a personal thing, but that God would show us something about the ministry of Heartbeat over there. However, before we were even to get our feet on the plane, we had to overcome many obstacles.

When God speaks to you and tells you to do something, it is at that point that the enemy will try everything to turn you away from your calling. You know that God has called, and yet it seems as though it would be easier to ignore that calling and bury your head in the sand. So often we need to fight our way through the difficulties and show God that no matter what, we will respond to what He is saying.

First of all, some in Heartbeat began to question our calling. Ray and I felt it was right to write a letter to Heartbeat's prayer partners and ask them to pray for us while we were in South Africa and also to give them the opportunity of helping us financially with the tickets. We had no money to go on this trip and we needed around £1,500 for the flights. However, some of the people in Heartbeat weren't sure if this was right, as they perceived our trip to be a personal vision and not a Heartbeat one. No matter how many times we said that we believed this trip would affect Heartbeat as a whole, it was not seen in that light. Ray and I felt disappointed, but we allowed the questions to push us back into God and continued to trust Him for the way ahead. We learned an important lesson at that point. It is important that when questions or obstacles to your faith arise, rather than backing off and running away from God, we should run into God and ask Him to continue to confirm His calling and show us the way ahead.

At the same time, the leader who had invited us to come on his trip seemed to change his mind. He phoned and left a long message on our voicemail saying that people in his team had been accusing us of muscling in on his trip. We phoned back and explained that the only reason we had booked our flights to coincide with his was because he had encouraged us to do so. We explained that we were setting up our own itinerary in South Africa, and that his co-ordinator had only booked our flights to and from South Africa. Unfortunately we could not change the tickets by then as the travel agency had confirmed them, otherwise we would have. The leader was receiving criticism from within his team because he had invited us when others within his church wanted to go. All these hassles added to our insecurity. Questions like 'Are we sure God has told us to go?' kept coming into our minds, but the more we prayed about it, the more God kept confirming that we were doing the correct thing. Money started to arrive in the post, our prayer partners were responding to the urgent need that we had, and soon we had received the £1,500 we needed for the journey.

At the same time, we were asking God where we should go when we got to South Africa. Our friends at Kingsway told us that if we were going to South Africa, we had to make sure that we met a man called Malcolm du Plessis, a leader of a church in Durban and well-known for his pioneering and creative ministry in the realm of praise and worship. We were also given the name of an English couple in Durban who, when we contacted them, said we could stay with them for a few days. It turned out that they knew us from a mission we had done previously in Oxfordshire. We were also given contacts in East London, Capetown and Johannesburg. As we prayed we felt God tell us to book a 'rover ticket', which would take us to Durban first, then East London, Capetown and then end up in Jo'burg.

It was a very nervous Ray and Nancy who boarded the plane in London. We did not see the people we were supposed to be travelling with until well into our journey. All the tension we felt just added to our insecurity.

When we arrived at Jo'burg, after a long flight from London, I remember a very funny incident happening to me. When we went to book our internal flight on to Durban, the guy at the check-in desk asked me to smile. I thought it was a strange thing to say, but I thought I'd better co-operate with his request, so I looked at him and smiled. The guy then asked again, and so again I beamed an even bigger smile back at him. It was only when Ray looked at me as if to say, 'What is wrong with you?' that I realised the guy behind the counter had not asked me to smile but had asked if I wanted a 'Smoking or non-smoking seat?' I felt such an idiot! I had totally misunderstood his accent. He must have wondered why this woman was just standing there grinning at him.

When we arrived in Durban we were taken to the home of Richard and Jill Lawton, the couple that had said we could stay with them. They were fantastic and made us feel so welcome. They even gave us their own bedroom to sleep in. They did not make any demands on us, but showered us with love and acceptance. Despite their very warm welcome, we still felt very insecure about being in South Africa. We kept asking ourselves, 'Why has God brought us here?' To make things worse, when we attended a church service in Durban people kept asking us why we had come to South Africa. When we answered, 'Well, we know this sounds really weird, but we came because we felt God tell us to come and that He would show us why when we got here.' The look of disbelief in their eyes was more than evident and again that added to our insecurity.

On the fourth day of being in Durban just before we were due to fly out to our next port of call, we met Malcolm du Plessis. He had just returned from a trip out of town but from the moment we set our eyes on Malcolm, we knew we would just love him. He is still the most unusual flamboyant person we know. However, we did not realise just how significant this meeting would be. He began to tell us about a band called 'Friends First', which he had founded. To our utter amazement we found that our vision and the vision that God had given him were almost identical. He had been responsible for getting together a group of multi-racial Christian singers and musicians to record an album as a prophetic challenge to the Church *and* to their nation. He told us that many churches had prayed and helped them financially with the project. They believed that God wanted to use them and their music to be a voice to their nation against the evil of apartheid. Their exciting music reached high in the secular charts at that time.

We began to tell him about the work of Heartbeat and how we had just completed a tour called 'Heal our Nation'. We told him about our half-night of prayer when God had met with us in such a clear way and told us about a 'tidal wave' of His Spirit coming to the land (this story is told in chapter 10). He excitedly told us that we must meet a friend of his called Joe Arthur, who was in the Friends First band and had produced all their singles and albums. We were thrilled to discover that Joe lived in Capetown as we were going there in a few days. Malcolm arranged to fly to Capetown and meet us there and introduce us to Joe. Before we left England, one of the most pressing needs in Heartbeat at the time was the need to find a producer who could produce our next album. We had tried to hire quite a number of people, but each one had not been able to do it in the time scale we had. After meeting Malcolm, Ray and I wondered if God had not only brought us to South Africa to sharpen our vision but also to meet the guy who would produce our next album.

When we arrived in Capetown we immediately really liked Joe and his wife Dee. We loved the vision and music of Friends First, and were very impressed with what we heard Joe producing. That night we prayed that somehow we would be able to meet Joe again and be able to chat with him some more about Heartbeat. When we discovered that we were all booked onto the same flight to fly to Jo'burg to go to the same concert, we just knew God was working behind the scenes and that this was a God-appointment. The four of us chatted at great length on the plane and when we asked Joe if he would come and produce our next album he immediately responded very positively. It was a miracle that he had the space in his diary and was willing to fly to England over the exact dates that we were able to book a studio over here.

On the way home on the plane we reflected on all that God had said and done and as we prayed we thanked Him for His amazing grace to us. We came home knowing that God was telling us that we must be a 'voice to the nation', and not just a 'voice to the church'. From that one trip to South Africa, we had our producer. Ray began to write, with others from Heartbeat, the song 'Voice to the Nation' and we were full of vision for the future.

Some of you reading this book will remember that we released a single into the charts called 'Tears from Heaven' from an album called *Voice to the Nation*. Joe produced both the album and the single. Our single was a song called 'Tears from Heaven' which reached number thirty-two in the pop charts in Britain and our band appeared on *Top of the Pops*. On our return from South Africa, Ray and I visited many if not all of the national Christian leaders of our country to ask if they would pray for us as we released what we believed was a prophetic single telling the nation that God cared for our land. We had amazing opportunities to share our faith with many of the national leaders of our land as well as to speak on national television and many radio programmes.

We could not believe how much had come out of one adventure of faith and how easy it would have been to stay at home. If we had submitted to our insecurities and given in to our problems and difficulties we would not have been at the right place at the right time. It was a learning time for all of us in Heartbeat, and although we all had to push through some reservations the team were fantastic at getting behind us and praying for us before and during our trip. On the plane on the way home, the Christian leader who had invited us to travel with him apologised for the problems we had encountered before we left and thanked us for the encouragement we had given him while he had been in South Africa.

If God has told you to do something, no matter how strong the opposition is against you, do make sure you obey God first and He will bring huge amounts of blessing from it. However, first of all you need to be sure that it is God who has spoken to you and not just your own thoughts or inclinations. There are many ways that God speaks to us; I have listed some in chapter

14. However, one of the most common ways in which God communicates with us is through the Bible. But if we are not reading His Word then it will be more difficult to hear His voice. I cannot emphasise enough how important it is to read the Bible. God has given us a wonderful book full of His instructions and promises and it is essential that we not only read it, but that we hide it in our hearts by memorising it. If God wants to speak to Ray and me, He will often do so by showing us something from His written Word. However, in all our walks of faith, as we have heard from God through the Bible, through the peace in our hearts, through hearing His still small voice, and through other people, we have found it was also important to submit what we feel we have heard to others who are wiser and more mature in their faith. If we are truly hearing from God then it will stand up to scrutiny, and submitting it to others will keep us from going in a wrong direction.

Exercises for your faith muscles

▶ Read Genesis 12:1–5. The Lord speaks to Abram and tells him to leave his home, his family and his nation and trust God to lead him to a new home. Take a few moments to think through how Abram must have felt. How would you feel if God asked you to do something similar? What can we learn from Abram's response to God?

▶ Read Genesis 21:9–20. Hagar too was sent on a journey, however before long we can see something of the problems and difficulties she encountered (Genesis 21:15–16). God sent an angel to her to open her eyes to His provision and His faithfulness to her and her son, Ishmael. Write down/discuss what we can learn from this.

▶ It is so important to hear God speak to us. Write down/discuss ways in which we can hear God speak to us and write down/discuss what we can do to develop this further.

▶ Memorise Isaiah 7:9b:

  'If you do not stand firm in your faith,
  you will not stand at all.'

Chapter 9

Hindrances to Faith

'A Christian should never say, "I can't afford it!" The question you need to ask is "Does God want me to have this?" If God wants you to have it, then you can afford it.'

Before Ray and I went into full-time Christian work, I remember an incident happening that taught us a lot about God and the fact that He wants each of us to exercise our faith in Him. Ray, as I mentioned earlier, was on tour with the Dave Pope band, and I had flown out to be with him for the last two weeks. Ray and I did not have very much money and had calculated out how much we had to spend each day. We were staying in the home of a lovely Christian couple. One day, our hosts' grown-up children asked us if we would like to go out with them for a meal. We said we would and we arranged a night to do so. As we discussed it, we knew that we only had a very small amount we could spend on a meal out and therefore we agreed that we would spend a certain amount but no more. We prayed that somehow we would have the right money for the meal. To be honest, I worried quite a bit about it and because of that could not really enjoy the night out. Both of us knew that we could not really afford to go out for a meal. When it came to ordering our meal, we ordered one meal and asked for two plates. Fortunately, that kind of practice is common in America and Canada as their portions are so big. We shared the meal and knew that after buying our main course our money had gone.

When the waitress came to ask us what we would like for dessert, we immediately declined declaring that we were full and could not possibly eat a pudding. Our friends pressed us again and again, but we knew we did not have enough money so we declined again and again. They went ahead and ordered amazing desserts and when they came, my mouth watered so much. They looked fantastic. A huge pint jug full of strawberries, ice cream and cream – my favourite and all I could do was to sit there and watch them eat it all. When it came time to get the bill, we took our carefully calculated finances out of our pockets, but our friends immediately said, 'Oh did we not tell you that this meal is on us?'

We learned several huge lessons that night. Firstly we learned that worry is a huge hindrance to faith. Jesus tells us quite clearly in Matthew 6:25 that we should not worry; yet it is so easy for the cares of this world to lodge themselves in our minds. Jesus even says, ' . . . *do not worry, saying, "What shall we eat?"* ' (Matthew 6:31). Yet fear and worry kept us from enjoying a special meal that God had ordered for us. I have, since this experience, memorised the following verse:

> '*Do not worry about anything; instead, pray about everything; tell God your needs and don't forget to thank him for his answers.*'   (Philippians 4:6 TLB)

I have to remind myself often about this verse because it is so easy to move from faith to worry. At one time not too long ago, I remember worrying about our future. Would God provide for us when we were old and grey and perhaps no longer able to do ministry? As I did what Philippians 4:6 tells us to do and presented my worries to God He spoke to me so clearly from 1 Kings:

> '*For this is what the* LORD, *the God of Israel, says: "The jar of flour will not be used up and the jug of oil will not run dry until the day the* LORD *gives rain on the land."*'
>   (1 Kings 17:14)

God spoke and said, 'Nancy, the jug of oil will not run dry. You do not need to worry about your latter years.' When we take our worries to God we can rest assured that He will deal with them.

The second thing we learned that night was that we should never say that we cannot afford something. First and foremost we must go to God and ask Him if He wants us to have it. If He does then we can certainly afford it! We have the richest Heavenly Father a person can have. Everything on this earth belongs to Him (Psalm 24:1). All we need to do is to listen and ask God what His instructions are so that we can see it all come into being.

Thirdly, we learned that once we heard from God we then needed to exercise our faith. Never once did we ask God what He wanted us to spend on that meal. All we knew was that what we had calculated was what we could afford and we asked God to keep it within our budget. We did not ask God what His budget was; if we had it would have been a different story. We restricted God's blessing on us by not believing Him for more. Both of us said we would never do that again.

We have a Heavenly Father who so longs to bless His children. I'm convinced that many of us do not receive what God has for us because we do not listen to God and then exercise our faith. Romans 10:17 tells us,

> ' . . . *faith comes from hearing the message, and the message is heard through the word of Christ.'*   (Romans 10:17)

Faith begins to stir in your heart when you hear God speak to you. Keep listening to God and get His perspective on your circumstances. Perhaps someone reading this book can identify with what happened to us in Canada. As we counted our pennies and restricted our budget, it seemed the correct thing to do. However, our decision was made without hearing from God and exercising our faith in Him. Perhaps you are not receiving the blessing of God because in some way you are restricting Him.

Just recently Ray, our boys Aidan and Daniel, and I went ten-pin bowling. Although I have been bowling many times with the boys, for some reason this time I damaged my arms. When I woke the next morning, one arm in particular was extremely painful and I could not move it in any direction. I discovered that not being able to use my arms restricted me in so many ways. I couldn't even get out of bed in the morning without Ray helping me out. I couldn't wash my hair, dress, write, use a computer and of course I couldn't drive. There were some other things I couldn't do either, which brought a smile to my face – like washing the dishes, making the meals, washing the clothes and cleaning up after my boys. All I could do was to sit, smile and watch, while Ray, Daniel and Aidan did all the chores. Although there were a few good points to me losing the use of my arms, it was very painful and I found it very restrictive. If we lose faith in God we will find that it also restricts us in our walk with God –

> *'If you do not stand firm in your faith,*
> *you will not stand at all.'* (Isaiah 7:9b)

Let me tell you about a good friend of mine who now works for ngm and who has a wonderful story of faith to tell. When I met Helen Pett she had been working for a company for seven years and although she was highly successful and earning a huge salary she told me she had lived for most of her working life in debt. She had also felt during a three-week holiday-of-a-lifetime in Thailand that her life was really a mess and that her relationship with God was not what it should be. After this holiday and just before she met me, in September 1995, she felt God speak to her and call her into full-time Christian work. She had felt God say that she should talk with me about the possibility of joining ngm. She knew that none of us in ngm had salaries as such, but that each of us 'lived by faith' and depended on God for our finances. It seemed such a huge step to take. If she ended up in debt when she had a huge salary, how was she going to survive with no salary coming in each month?

She knew the only way forward was to hear clearly from God about the future. As she prayed and asked God to confirm His call, she received many encouraging words from the Scriptures. One of those scriptures really impacted her life. She read from Job 22:

> *'Submit to God and be at peace with him;*
> *in this way prosperity will come to you.*
> *Accept instruction from his mouth*
> *and lay up his words in your heart.*
> *If you return to the Almighty, you will be restored:*
> *If you remove wickedness far from your tent*
> *and assign your nuggets to the dust,*
> *your gold of Ophir to the rocks in the ravines,*
> *then the Almighty will be your gold,*
> *the choicest silver for you.*
> *Surely then you will find delight in the Almighty . . . '*
>
> (Job 22:21–26)

She knew that God was speaking to her and that He was promising to supply all her needs if she would put Him first. She gave in her notice and handed her life over to God.

As she joined ngm she received a huge shock when the firm she had worked for contacted her and told her that she had a debt owing to them for the remainder of a loan she had been given to buy a car. As you can imagine she was horrified. How was she going to pay off this debt now that she no longer had a salary? Her debt seemed such a hindrance to the future God had planned for her. They asked her to go back and work for them until the loan was paid but she knew that wasn't what God wanted. She immediately shared her problems with some of us at ngm and we prayed for God to move in supernatural power. During that night, one of the girls in ngm was woken up with a word from Psalm 18 for Helen:

> *'He reached down from on high and took hold of me;*
> *he drew me out of deep waters.*

He rescued me from my powerful enemy,
  from my foes, who were too strong for me.
They confronted me in the day of my disaster,
  but the LORD was my support.
He brought me out into a spacious place;
  he rescued me because he delighted in me.'

(Psalm 18:16–19)

When she received that word, although God had not yet answered, she felt such a release of faith in her heart. By the end of that week, every penny she needed to repay the loan had been miraculously supplied. God was indeed faithful and true to His Word.

Isn't it amazing that while she was receiving a salary of thousands of pounds, she could not get out of debt; but when she put her life into the hands of Almighty God, despite having no salary and very little money, she was able to pay off all her debts. There is no problem too difficult for God and if we put Him first in our lives, He will honour and bless us.

Another girl who had worked on and off for ngm for a number of years came to us one day and said she felt that she wanted to move back to Thornbury and base herself with us as she pursued an opening into the media as a presenter. We talked about the possibility of her working with ngm on a part-time basis whilst pursuing any media opportunities as they came up. She had mentioned that she had some debts to pay off and as such she wondered whether she needed to get a job to pay them off.

We encouraged her not to rush into getting a paid job just because that seemed to be the obvious way of getting finance. It is not that we are against people working for a salary but we just wanted her to be sure that it was God's plan for her at this time. When we next spoke with her a couple of days later however, she had already acquired a part-time job as a sales assistant. Before long she was offered a full-time post as the manager of the shop. A number of months later we noticed that she didn't seem to have enough time, because of her job, to be able to pursue her dream of working for God through the media. When we talked with her about this we also discovered that not only was she not able to pursue her dream, but her debts were increasing instead of decreasing. Here she was in a well paid job and yet instead of getting free from debt – which was the reason she took the job – however hard she tried she was getting more and more bogged down by debt. As we prayed with her it became obvious that instead of her depending on her job to get her out of debt, she needed to depend on God. It seemed crazy to be leaving a good salaried job but we agreed together to stand in faith for these debts to be removed. We also felt that as she pursued God for her future, He would open the doorway to see the prophetic words that had been spoken into her life (that she would work in the media as a presenter) come into being. We told her we would stand with her and together combine our faith in God to see this happen.

Within a month of her leaving her job not only did God supply her with the finances she needed to live on, but He also provided enough money to pay off all her debts. When we have faith as small as a mustard seed and we do what God wants us to do, we see miracles happen. By the way, she is working today as a presenter on television. Our God is indeed faithful.

It is extremely easy these days to get into debt. Every day I receive one or two envelopes inviting me to acquire a personal loan. We only have to listen and look at the television adverts that try and convince us that we could buy that car, have that new kitchen, go on that wonderful idyllic holiday, if only we would take a loan from them. They tell us the whole process is painless and easy but what is not said is that it can be very difficult to eventually get out of debt. The latest figures from the Bank of England tell us that in the nation of Britain today we have personal debts of billions. We owe £50.19 billion on plastic cards, £164.37 billion on all unsecured debt and £713.78 billion on mortgages (taken from a report by Richard Palmer and Sarah O'Grady in the *Daily Express* 2nd August 2003). What the loan companies don't tell us is that although they are giving us a certain sum of money, we will be paying them a huge amount of money back. I am not suggesting for a moment that *all* loans are wrong; many of us have mortgages on our homes and in the Bible we are encouraged to lend to others (Deuteronomy 15:8; Psalms 37:26; 112:5). However, it makes financial sense to only borrow what you know you can expect to repay. In all these areas we should go to God first for His wisdom and make sure we hear and obey what He is saying. Personally I believe it is important never to get into debt without having the equity to repay it.

In ngm we do not encourage people to have overdrafts or to use credit cards unless they know God has already given them the means to pay it back. It is so easy to have faith in your credit card or in an overdraft rather than have your faith in God. When we have a bill, do we automatically go to God and ask Him what He wants us to do? Or do we just write the cheque, or put the bill on our credit card, and then forget about it? By doing so we are restricting God and not allowing Him to speak to us about the situation.

I remember recently giving that challenge at an ngm meeting, and being surprised at the many people who had the courage that night to admit that they had put more faith in their credit card and overdraft facilities than they had in God. If you find yourself in this position, do spend time asking God what He wants you to do. Don't assume that this teaching only applies to people who are in so-called 'full-time' Christian work – this is for everyone. Each one of us, whether we have a salary or not, should be living by faith and depending on God for all our needs. It says quite clearly in Hebrews 11:6 that *'without faith it is impossible to please God'*. God did not mean that we should have faith in one area (perhaps to see a friend become a Christian) and not in another area (personal finances, etc.). God wants us all to trust Him and have faith in Him in every area of our lives, including finances.

Just recently, without Ray and me knowing it, our son Daniel prayed and asked God for a set of drums. He had a passion to be a drummer and although he had spoken of that desire, neither

Ray nor I really knew how deep it went. One night, after Ray had spoken at one of our ngm meetings, he called people forward who were believing God for something that had not yet come into being. A number of people responded including Daniel. Ray prayed for them and asked God to bring into being those things that did not exist at this moment in time. As Daniel went back to his seat at the back of the venue, a young guy called Joe who is the drummer in the ngm band 'Steve' approached Daniel and asked him if he was still looking for a set of drums. When Daniel answered in the affirmative, Joe then said 'I've got a set of drums that you can have. I felt from God that I should give them to you.' As you can imagine, Daniel was overjoyed. It does not matter who you are, whether you are young or old, working for God or working for an earthly employer, God expects us to live out and exercise our faith. When you do, watch out for the miracles to happen.

Over the years we have had people question and criticise the way we live. We don't mind people asking questions, but when people criticise without speaking to you or understanding your circumstances it can really be a hindrance to your faith. I remember one girl's church would not support her financially when she came to ngm because the church felt that we should be paying her for what she was doing. They felt the way we lived was unbiblical and told her to stop trying to sponge off everyone else. Not only were their comments very hurtful to that girl but their theology was also quite wrong. It is quite clear from the Bible that Jesus Himself lived by faith and depended on others for finance (Luke 8:3).

Critical words can be very damaging to faith. Rather than criticise it would have been more helpful if that church had asked Ray and myself why we live this way. If they had, they would have discovered that we don't have anything against salaries or being paid for what we do but that God has quite clearly told us in ngm to depend on Him for our finances and not to depend on a salary structure as such.

When God told us to leave British Youth for Christ and begin to depend on Him for finances, we knew that He was telling us to keep close to Him. When we have a need, whether financial or otherwise, we should go to Him first and foremost to ask for His instructions. If He tells us to write and mention our needs to our prayer partners then that is what we will do. If He tells us not to tell anyone, again, this is what we will do. If He tells us to go and directly ask someone if they can help us in our faith walk, then again that is what we will do. Listening closely to God is of utmost importance to our life of faith. I have to say that during the time I have lived this way I have had more money, gifts and holidays from my Heavenly Employer than I ever would have had from an earthly employer.

Someone also said to that girl when she mentioned that she was now living by faith, 'Don't you mean dying by faith?' They expected us all to die by faith and not have the means to live. I can tell you from over 24 years of experience of living this way and seeing God provide, not only for us but also for the whole of ngm, that we are certainly not 'dying by faith'. That doesn't mean that we don't have days where we don't know where we are going to get our next penny from, it just means that when we do have a need, we know where to go to find life. Over the years Ray and I have been so encouraged by those who have given to us regularly to enable us to do the work God has called us to do. People have sacrificially given us finance and gifts just at the right time. Their generosity does not go unnoticed by us or by our Heavenly Father. Money, at times, has been pushed into our hands; holidays given to us; and clothes paid for. Even when we were on a plane in South Africa, a lady who I had started to speak to during the journey to Capetown pushed 20-rand into my hand just before I got off the plane. There have been many times when we haven't had money to buy what we would have wanted but we always had enough money for what we needed. There have been times when we were on holiday in Santa Ponsa in Majorca (at the generosity of George and Jean Sinclair, two leaders from our church in Scotland who owned an apartment there), and only had enough money to share a pizza, side salad and a coke between us each day for our main meal – but it was all we needed at the time. We've experienced many lean times as well as times of enormous blessing.

In Heartbeat days, whenever one person was hurting financially, we all went to prayer asking God why. We knew that God only needed to stop the finances coming in and He had our fullest attention. Whatever God said through our prayer time we would then put into practice through obedience. We would also take up an offering from within ourselves to help the person in their walk of faith. We always felt that unless God specifically said, 'don't give in this instance because I want to provide in another way', we would always give what we could to help. This is a principle we have tried to encourage throughout the years, even though we have grown in numbers.

I remember once not having enough money to pay our babysitter. When we went out to the ngm meetings we often asked a young guy from the local church in Malmesbury if he would babysit for our son, Daniel. We always paid him £5 for doing so. This particular night we did not have £5 in our bank account to give him so we prayed and asked God somehow to give us the money. When we returned from our ngm meeting Ray and I showed our babysitter our new Heartbeat album. The album had just been released and as each member of Heartbeat got a free copy, Ray and I came home with two copies between us. As no money had arrived, I opened our chequebook and prayed that God would somehow let us have the money in our account by the time the cheque was cashed. Just as I lifted my pen to write, our babysitter suddenly said. 'I hope you don't mind me asking, but rather than give me a cheque tonight, would you mind if I had a copy of your album instead?' Relief flooded through us as we realised that God had answered our prayers right at the last moment. We did not need two copies of our album, we only needed one and it was a joy to give the other copy away.

I remember another lady declaring to us after we had enjoyed a holiday week in Spain that 'missionaries don't have holidays'. Many people feel that those who are in the ministry – pastors, missionaries and Christian workers – should all be kept poor. I have heard people get extremely upset and annoyed at church business meetings because they thought their pastor was getting too much money. Yet the pastor's salary was not as much as the average person in the church was receiving from their employment. 1 Timothy tells us that,

> *'The elders who direct the affairs of the church well are worthy of double honour, especially those whose work is preaching and teaching.'* (1 Timothy 5:17)

The Bible also states in Luke 10:7 and 1 Corinthians 9:8 that a workman is worthy of his hire and that we should not muzzle an ox while it is treading out the grain. Let's not make it extra difficult for those who serve us in the house of the Lord. Generosity is something that should be encouraged, after all we have an amazingly generous Heavenly Father and we are exhorted in the Bible to become more like Him. Psalm 37:26 tells us that the righteous are always generous; Psalm 112:5 promises that good will come to those who are generous; Proverbs 11:25 and 22:9 both tell us that a generous person will themselves be blessed and refreshed and will prosper.

We are encouraged in the Bible to:

> *'store up for yourselves treasures in heaven, where moth and rust do not destroy, and where thieves do not break in and steal.'* (Matthew 6:20)

I remember Ray and me hearing a man preaching while we were visiting South Africa who had thousands if not millions of pounds go through his hands. He made it his practice to give away money to someone every day of his life. He would ask God whom He wanted to bless on that day and then was obedient to what God was saying. He discovered that as he gave out, God poured in more so that he had even more to give away. A saying of his has stuck in our minds over the years. He said, 'You cannot take your money with you to heaven, but you can send it on ahead.' He was a man who realised that his heavenly bank account was more important than his earthly one.

One of the things we have done in ngm throughout the years is to give to the poor and to other Christian workers and organisations. We have also been on the receiving end when other Christian organisations have given gifts of finance to us. When we first set up our ngm bank account in 1983 we felt God tell us to give a tithe of our money to others who were doing a similar work to us. Not only would we be sowing into their ministry, but we also knew it would help to destroy any unbiblical competition that might arise in us.

Another hindrance to faith is fear. I heard a story that appeared in a newspaper years ago about a lady who had been invited to attend a conference in New York. Although this was long before the September 11th tragedies, she was fearful of travelling to that city because of all the violence, crime and mugging that she knew went on there. However, because she desperately wanted to go, she decided to book herself into one of the top hotels in New York, thinking she would be safe there.

On the night she arrived, she went down to the restaurant to have her meal. Halfway through her meal, it suddenly dawned on her that she had left her handbag in her bedroom. So leaving her meal, she went back upstairs in the lift to her bedroom where thankfully she discovered her bag was safe and sound. She again locked her bedroom door and then called the lift. When the lift doors opened, inside the lift were three rather large black gentlemen. All sorts of thoughts were going through her mind in the few seconds she had to make up her mind what to do. She thought to herself, 'Oh no, should I get into the lift with these three men – will they mug me?' Then she thought to herself, 'Well, they have seen me now; I'd better go in.' She walked into the lift and immediately turned her back on the three gentlemen.

As the lift doors closed a gruff voice said, 'Hit the floor, lady.'

In that moment, all her fears were realised. She got down on her hands and knees and threw her handbag behind her saying, 'Don't hurt me, please don't hurt me, take my money, but please don't hurt me.'

There was silence for a few seconds and then the men began to laugh.

As they gently lifted her to her feet they explained, 'What we meant was hit the floor, push the button – what floor do you want?'

As she went to eat the rest of her meal she was really embarrassed and could not believe what she had done. When she called the waitress to ask if she could sign for her meal, she was told that three gentlemen had paid her bill. She thought that was a very kind gesture, but then when she came to collect her bill after staying in the hotel a whole week, she was told that she had nothing to pay. She couldn't understand it, however the receptionist told her that a gentleman had paid her bill and had left her a note. When she opened it, she read the following, 'Thanks for the greatest laugh I have had in years' – and it was signed by Eddie Murphy.

She had managed to mistake Eddie Murphy and his two minders for three muggers. Her fear had caused her to make a hugely embarrassing mistake.

Although this is a funny story, fear can stop us not only enjoying our walk of faith, but also receiving all that God has for us. I mentioned in the introduction chapter about God asking Ray and myself to approach my brother and tell him, 'The Lord has need of your car.' My fear of the reaction from my brother and my parents stopped us enjoying a holiday in Weston-super-Mare that we badly needed, and almost stopped us from doing what God had told us to do. When Ray first stepped out in faith and believed God for healing, he had to first overcome his fear of failure and of God not turning up. When God called us, Ray struggled with the fear of telling his parents that he was leaving their family business and moving to live in England. Fear, if not dealt with, can leave us paralysed and devoid of faith. In any walk of faith we will always have to overcome our fears.

We had to overcome many fears during 1984 when God took

us on a faith journey to receive a new car. When God told us He was going to give us a brand new car we were absolutely thrilled because the car we had at that time was a rather beaten-up Ford Cortina which kept breaking down. It was always really embarrassing. We would arrive at a school where we would take an assembly, classes and a lunchtime concert. When we finished the team would all pile into the van and the car and head for our next venue. More often than not, we had to get out of the car and push it to get it started, much to the amusement of the watching school-kids!

We shared what we felt God was saying with people we respected in God, in order to check that we had heard God right. It is always scary yet exciting to start a new walk of faith. We began with only a word from God, no money and no idea of how God was going to provide. As we prayed we received a number of small gifts through the post and our faith and trust started to grow. We then prayed and asked God to help us sell our old car, as we were about to embark on a three-month national tour with BYFC, which would mean our car hardly being used. We could barely contain our excitement when we sold the car a week or two later for the exact amount of money we had asked for. We even told the person who was buying our car all its faults, including the fact that it broke down each time it stopped, but he still wanted it! We knew that selling our car was a real miracle in itself and that encouraged us to believe God for more. Not only that, but some people we knew phoned and offered us the loan of a car until we were able to purchase our own. As we continued to pray throughout the tour, the money kept coming in. While on tour we were astounded when one of the artists who was working with us gave us a gift of a thousand pounds specifically earmarked for our new car.

We then asked God if He would put us in touch with a businessman who could help us get a good deal on a new vehicle. During the next part of the tour we stayed with some good friends of ours, Ian and Marjorie Frith. During the course of conversation, Ian and Marjorie asked us what we were praying for at that moment in time. When we told them that we were asking God to bring us in touch with someone who could help us get a brand new car for a very good price, we were genuinely amazed when they said they could help. Ian was a businessman who had a good relationship with his local garage and he volunteered to help us get a brand new car for a much-reduced price. As God was continuing to answer our prayers, we explored what kind of car we should buy. In the end we picked a Maestro, which would cost around £5,500. As we already had £3,500, we didn't feel it would be long before we would be ordering our new car.

After a few weeks, Ian phoned us one day and asked if we wanted to go ahead and order the car. Ray and I sent up a few quick prayers and then said yes, hoping that we had done the right thing. It was only after we had put the phone down that it dawned on us that we had ordered the car, without having all the finance we needed. However, once we had spent time praying, our fears were once again put to rest. God had been so faithful to us; we just needed to trust Him for the rest of the journey. As the day came closer for Ray to go to Birmingham to collect the car, fear started raising its ugly head again in our hearts. What if God did not provide? We had received some more money, but we did not have enough to cover the complete bill.

On the day when Ray had to take a train to Birmingham to collect the car, we did not have the full amount we needed. What would Ian say when Ray arrived in Birmingham without having the full amount of money? Fear had us panicking and it was only as we prayed and asked God for His faith that we felt Ray should go and we should trust that God would somehow provide. While Ray travelled to Birmingham, I was at home having a long conversation with God. I could not understand what God was doing. To be honest, I felt let down by God. Hadn't God said that He was going to give us a new car? Why had He not provided? My deadline to get the money had passed and God had not brought into being what He had said He would do. I was angry with God and I remember unloading all my complaints onto Him as I vacuumed the carpet. I didn't realise it at the time, but the enemy was undermining God's word again and again. I was focusing in on my fears rather than trusting in God to increase my faith.

My anger eventually evaporated and as I sat down on the couch I asked God to speak to me. I opened my Bible and the first verse my eyes saw was from Matthew:

> '. . . *with God all things are possible.*'   (Matthew 19:26)

I knew God was speaking to me and I immediately repented and apologised for my fear, my anger and my lack of faith. I thanked God that with Him all things are possible and told Him I would continue to trust Him. When I had finished I noticed that my Bible had fallen shut. As I wiped away the tears from my eyes, I opened my Bible again and this time the first verse I saw was from Mark:

> '*Everything is possible for him who believes.*'   (Mark 9:23)

I never advocate opening your Bible and taking potluck, as it were, but it was almost as though God had put those two verses in bold in my Bible. They jumped out of the pages at me. Fear was suddenly gone as I realised that God was still in control and if I trusted Him He would bring His promise into being. Suddenly my joy returned and there was a lightness in my spirit.

While this was happening to me, Ray was heading to the train station to embark on his journey to Birmingham. He had read several stories in books about people who needed finance from God who suddenly met someone on a train or a bus who then put into their hands the exact amount they needed. So, full of anticipation, he boarded his train for Birmingham and sat down and waited for his messenger from God! At the next station, a man got on and sat opposite Ray. Within a couple of minutes, he looked over at Ray and said, 'Are you a Christian?' Ray thought to himself, 'This is it!' and could see pound signs

in the man's eyes before he answered with a rather expectant,
'Yes'.

The man had noticed Ray's Youth for Christ sticker on his
briefcase and started chatting to him about what God was
doing in mainland Europe. God had been talking to us at that
point in our ministry about expanding our work to Europe, but
as this man talked Ray was experiencing some head noise.
Inside his head, Ray was shouting to God, 'Yes, Lord, I hear you
about Europe; but where is our money?' You can imagine the
disappointment in Ray's spirit as the man got off at the next
station without giving him a penny! Again, fear started to creep
in. What was Ian going to say when Ray did not have enough
money? As the train got nearer and nearer to Birmingham,
Ray battled with fear of failure and fear of rejection. As he
quietly prayed he realised afresh that it was impossible for God
to let us down and told God he would trust Him despite the
circumstances.

Ray met Ian at the station and then both of them went to the
garage to collect the car. As Ray took out his cheque book,
praying that somehow God would enlarge our bank balance,
Ian said, 'Don't worry about that just yet. Did you think you
needed to pay for the car today? What will happen is that the
garage will invoice me and then I will invoice you, but the
whole process will take several months.' Relief flooded through
Ray as he realised God had stepped in.

The more I've gone on with God, the more I've realised that
my deadlines are not always the same as God's deadlines. We
once heard Ian Andrews make a very true statement, 'Your
faith walk begins when you think it should end.' We thought
we had to pay the bill when we collected the car but God knew
otherwise. Ray came home with a brand new car and we hadn't
needed to pay a penny! When we paid the bill several months
later we had received enough money to cover the total cost.
Fear could have stopped us from receiving all that God had for
us, but it was as we clung to God and faced our fears that our
faith increased enough to believe God for His promises.

I met a lady called Paula recently who won't allow fear of

other people's reactions to stop her from obeying God. One day whilst fasting she heard God ask her to make a chicken casserole. She wondered to herself if God was going to direct someone to her house for dinner that evening, but when no one appeared she prayed again and the name of a family who lived down the road came into her mind. Despite the embarrassment she was feeling, she got into her car with her chicken casserole and drove to her friends' home. When the wife answered the door, Paula held out the casserole and the words 'I have brought tomorrow's dinner' fell out of her mouth. The family was overjoyed as they had just finished praying and asking God to provide tomorrow's food.

At another point in her life, Paula felt God tell her to take a brand new toothbrush to a friend's home. You can imagine how she felt as she rang the doorbell with her toothbrush in her hand. When her friend came to the door she said, 'I know this sounds bizarre, but I felt God tell me to bring this toothbrush to you.' Her friend was so surprised as someone had just come to stay and had forgotten their toothbrush. Paula had to overcome her embarrassment and fear on both these occasions but as she was obedient, God used her intimacy with Him to show His love and care to others.

When we step out on a faith walk with God, there will be many hindrances to our faith, but God encourages us to,

> '... *fix our eyes on Jesus, the author and perfecter of our faith.*'
> (Hebrews 12:2)

As it says in the previous verse, let's throw off everything that hinders us and let's keep running in faith with God. As we do, He will increase our faith to believe Him for more.

Exercises for your faith muscles

▶ Here is a list of a number of hindrances to our faith. Go through the list slowly and see if you can identify with having any of these in your heart:

- Worry
- Fear
- Unbelief
- Debt
- Sin
- Discouragement
- False picture of God
- Low self-image
- Presumption
- Criticism
- Failure

► Find a verse in the Bible that tells us what we should do with each hindrance.

► Meditate on Hebrews 12:1 and discuss or write down what God says.

► Memorise Hebrews 12:1:

> *'Therefore, since we are surrounded by such a great crowd of witnesses, let us throw off everything that hinders and the sin that so easily entangles, and let us run with perseverance the race marked out for us.'*

The very first
Heartbeat (left–right):
Dave, Nancy, Ray,
Jackie, Colin and
Jonny.

Glimpse of revival in
Preston where over
500 responded to the
gospel.

Producer Joe Arthur
(right) from South
Africa, recording our
Voice to the Nation
album.

Heartbeat in the late 80s (left–right from top): Ray, Sue, Steve, Carl, Nancy, Dave, Clive, Sarah and Su.

Taken at Peterborough during Kingdom Faith week where many were saved and healed.

Young people responding at a Heartbeat concert.

An early Heartbeat photo (left–right from top): Trish, Dave, Dorry, Ian, Ray and Nancy.

Nancy on stage at an early Heartbeat concert.

Our first miracle van.

Extracts from Heartbeat newsletters in the 80s.

Heartbeat's first offices.

New ngm missions and arts complex.

ngm DJ and worship leader Andy Hunter on main stage at Festival Manchester 2003.

ngm band Steve leading worship at Festival Manchester 2003.

Chapter 10

Revival Faith

'I looked and I saw a mighty tidal wave heading towards the shores of our land. As the wave broke, it quickly spread throughout the whole nation, and as I watched, God spoke. "I am sending a new wave of My Spirit to this land, bringing healing, justice and forgiveness. The time is near and I want My people to get ready, pray and prepare themselves for what I am about to do." '

One day during 1985 when Ray was out walking and talking to God, he felt God encourage him to start to pray for the nation as a whole. At that point Ray and I were leading the band, Heartbeat, and so we decided to ask the others to join us as we began to regularly pray for the nation of Britain.

As we had travelled extensively throughout the island of Britain, we were well aware of the state of our nation. Crime was on the increase; abuse – both physical and sexual – of children was common. Old ladies were being mugged, raped and sometimes left for dead. The number of people having abortions had increased and a large percentage of teenagers had slept with someone by the time they had reached sixteen. More and more people were becoming homeless and there was much racial tension. We only had to look in our newspapers to discover that our society was in a dreadful mess.

However, it was only when we asked God the following questions: 'How do You see our nation?' and 'How do You feel about our nation?' that we broke down and wept. God began to show us how heavy His heart was at the sin and sorrow He saw every day. We began to pour out our tears to God and repent on behalf of the nation, telling God how sorry we were that we had turned our backs on Him.

During one of our half-nights of prayer, when there was a real sense of expectancy, God began to speak powerfully through visions and prophetic words. In a vision, I saw an incredibly huge tidal wave, coming in towards the shores of our land. As the wave broke it crashed on to England and spread out to encompass the whole of Britain and went into other nations too. God spoke to me and said, 'I am bringing a new wave of My Spirit to this land. I am going to be doing something new and fresh by My Spirit, and thousands are going to be swept into My Kingdom. I want My people to pray and prepare for what I am about to do, but even if some of My people don't pray or prepare – I am coming anyway.'

What a God we've got! It is not as though we deserve revival, but God in His grace and mercy extends His love towards us. The vision God gave us that evening has become central to everything we do in ngm. Everything in our ministry now comes out of the conviction that God is going to pour out His Spirit in these last days in a huge and mighty way. We don't know how He is going to do it nor when it will happen but we do know that God is calling us, His Church to be prepared and ready for all He is going to do.

There was a sense in my heart that preparation needed to be inward as well as outward. God wanted His people to purge out anything that was within them that was not of Him. He also wanted us to have a *big* vision of what He wanted to do. I was reminded that evening of a scene I saw in Spain a few years earlier, while Ray and I were there on holiday.

We had been walking along a street in a small village when we noticed a huge crowd of people trying to get into a large church building. As we drew closer we noticed that the church was absolutely full and that many people couldn't get in. We wondered what was going on, as you don't usually see churches packed to capacity like that. We got as near as we could and peered into the building to discover that it was just a man at the front, preaching. We don't know what he was saying as he was speaking in Spanish; however God spoke to us very clearly at that moment. We felt Him saying that the time would come when the churches in Britain would be too small for what He was going to do. There would come a time when churches would be packed and people just wouldn't be able to get in. With conviction in our hearts, we said, 'Yes, Lord – do it!'

Around that time we had begun to see little glimpses of what we still believe God wants to do. In 1985 we held a three-week evangelistic mission in Preston. After chatting to the church leaders in Preston, we decided to hire the Charter Hall for five consecutive nights. Until that point, we normally held one evening event after a school or university mission, but this time we felt it was right to hold five evening events at the Charter Theatre which held 800 people. Obviously it was such a huge step of faith and there were times when we thought – 'What have we done?' However, what happened left us all quite amazed. During a couple of weeks in schools, colleges and universities we invited all the people we met to come to the Charter Theatre to see God's power in action. After one of our prayer meetings for the event, about two hours before the first event started, I went out of the theatre to pay a quick visit to the shops in the arcade below. What I saw as I left the theatre will be forever ingrained in my mind. Hundreds of people were already queuing all the way down the stairs to get in. Such was the hunger to know about God. They knew it was a Christian event where they would be given an opportunity to give their lives to Christ. Outside there was a huge banner over the theatre, which said 'God's power in action'. They weren't just coming to hear a band, they wanted to know if God was real and how He could affect their lives. These were scenes of which we had only read about in books on revival.

About half an hour before the concert was due to start, we

were already asking the Christians in the hall to leave and go to another room where they could pray for the event. That night over 100 responded as Ray gave the appeal to come to know Christ. Many were also healed as signs and wonders followed the preaching of the Word. Every night was electric and during the five evening events, each night was packed to capacity. Hundreds came to know the Lord. People were even being saved and healed in the overflow prayer meetings.

One particular story really stuck in my memory. A girl who had heard us in her school, decided to ask her Mum and Dad who were divorced to come to the concert with her. They sometimes did things together as a family for their daughter's sake. A word of knowledge was given about someone who was divorced and at the end of the event they and their daughter gave their lives to Jesus and asked for counsel to put their marriage back together again. When revival comes to our nation, thousands will turn to Christ; we need to be ready to help them to go from decisions to disciples.

In November of that same year we visited a town called Thornbury which would eventually, many years later, become the place where we would have our base. At the invitation of the local churches, we visited three schools in the area and then rented out the Armstrong Hall for the last night. Our newsletter reported what happened like this.

> 'Friday night saw the Armstrong Hall in Thornbury over-flowing. Every available seat had been taken and sadly, over 100 teenagers had to be turned away. It still amazes us that although everyone is told that they are coming to more than a concert and that they will hear us share our faith and explain what it is to be a Christian and give people an opportunity to respond, they still flock in to hear the good news. Over 70 responded. On the Sunday morning at the local church, one fourteen-year-old girl said, since becoming a Christian on the Friday night, she had felt clean on the inside and said it felt as though she had had a bath on the inside.'

On another of our missions – this time in 1984 – the headline on our newsletter was 'Christians asked to leave'. The report went something like this . . .

'Over one hundred Christians had to give up their seats at our final concert held recently at the end of a week of evangelism in Stroud. The final night was held in the biggest public hall available and twenty minutes before the concert began, the hall was absolutely packed. We finally had to ask the Christians if they would leave and go to the counselling room to pray, but even so we still had to turn away around 100 people. More than a hundred stood as Ray gave the appeal for people to follow Jesus. Quite a number were also healed as God confirmed His Word in a demonstration of His power. One man in particular told us afterwards how he had come to the evening in real pain as he had a disc complaint in his back. He explained how he felt the power of God go through him and how both the complaint and the pain disappeared. He then touched his toes to show the remarkable change in his condition.'

At one of our camps in 1985, we could not quite believe what we were seeing God do during our week in Newark. Our newsletter report reads like this:

'Words cannot express what we saw God do during the week. Non-Christians became Christians. People were set free from bondage. Many were filled with the Holy Spirit. The gifts of the Spirit were released in many people, gifts of tongues, prophecy, words of knowledge, numerous healings and miracles. There was repentance and recommitment to Christ. The power of God fell so heavily at times that the events inside the tent became like scenes from some of the past revivals: people weeping and getting right with God; many lost in worship and adoration, singing and speaking out in tongues; some kneeling and lying prostrate while others fell to the floor as the power of the Holy Spirit came upon them.'

During the '80s we saw many glimpses of revival that led us to cry out to God to move in such an awakening that the whole nation would be affected by what He was doing. It was important at that time to remember that God had said that we as a church needed to pray.

On one of our missions in Worcester God spoke clearly to us about the need to pray. With the backing of several churches and after a year-long foundation of prayer, we spent a week in Worcester presenting the message of Jesus. The aim for the mission was to make a real impact on the whole community. Richard Wood, the local co-ordinator at the time, had worked extremely hard and there was a real air of expectancy as the week arrived. We organised a two-hour prayer meeting every day for the mission but were disappointed when only a few people from the local area turned up. However, all that was about to change!

On our opening night we discovered that the local electricity board had wired the 1,300-seat hall incorrectly which meant we had to hire a generator. This arrived late and we were soon faced with a massive PA and lighting rig, an audience queuing up outside and experienced engineers frantically trying to get power. No matter what was tried the generator would not work. Our first reaction was to blame the enemy for disrupting the mission, but there was an inexplicable sense in our hearts that God was in this. When we realised that we were not going to get power that evening, we asked all the Christians in the audience to stay and gave out tickets to the rest to guarantee them seats for another night. What happened next was quite incredible.

As Ray led us in a time of prayer a local Christian man shared that he felt people needed to be praying and not just relying on ngm (Heartbeat) to do their part. As he spoke, Christians all over the hall started to repent. People, including leaders and pastors, were on their knees crying on God to forgive them and to bring revival. The prayer meeting went on for some time as God broke through. Earlier in the day, when only a few people had turned up for the prayer meeting, Ray and I had wondered what it would take to get the Christians praying. We never imagined that God would turn off the electricity! The very next morning we heard from our engineers that everything was working and that during the night the system appeared to have 'fixed itself'. The daily prayer meetings were amazing with over 100 people praying together. As we prayed, many who had come to pray saw God move in their lives in incredible ways – with one person getting out of a wheelchair and walking as God healed them.

During our time in Worcester we saw the 1,300-seat hall packed each night, with over 400 giving their lives to Christ and God touching many Christians in a deep way. Many were healed of physical and emotional hurts and at least one drug addict was completely set free. One incident really sticks in my memory. When Ray began to give the appeal at the end of the preach, a young teenage girl got up immediately and ran to the front in floods of tears and knelt down on the floor. When she was questioned as to her urgency, she said that she'd heard Jesus calling her name during the evening and could not wait to give her life to Him.

If we want to see God move in revival power in our nation and see scenes like these in our towns and in our cities, then we need to pray. When people pray and we add a measure of faith and obedience, amazing things can happen. God gave me a vision of revival in 1985 and I believe that although we have seen amazing moves of God throughout the '80s, we are now in the days when God wants to move with much more power. I am so convinced that there is a tidal wave of His Spirit coming and that if we want to be involved in what God wants to do in our nation, in Europe and in many of the nations of the world, then we need to get down on our knees and pray. We need to pray like we have never prayed before and reach out in faith and obedience to God. We need to start making friendships which will lead to many of our friends, family and the people we meet in our everyday lives coming to know the Lord. The song Ray and others in Heartbeat wrote out of that half-night of prayer in 1985 is called 'Heal our Nation'. Use this song as a basis for your prayers and let's fuel our faith to see God move in our land in supernatural power.

Heal our Nation

Lord we long for you to move in power
There's a hunger deep within our hearts
To see healing in our nation
Send your Spirit to revive us.

*Heal our Nation
Heal our Nation
Heal our Nation
Pour out your Spirit in this land.*

Lord, we hear your Spirit coming closer
A mighty wave to break upon our land
Bringing justice and forgiveness
God we cry to you, 'Revive us.'

(Trish Morgan; Ray Goudie; Ian Townend;
Dave Bankhead. Copyright © Thank You Music)

Exercises for your faith muscles

▶ Spend some time asking God how He feels about your nation.

▶ Ask God what He would like you to do personally to see your nation, your town, your neighbourhood and your friends impacted with the message and love of Jesus. Write down and obey what He says.

▶ Pray regularly for revival in yourself, your family, friends and neighbours.

► Memorise Isaiah 44:3:

> *'For I will pour water on the thirsty land,*
> *and streams on the dry ground;*
> *I will pour out my Spirit on your offspring,*
> *and my blessing on your descendants.'*

Chapter 11

Faith Obeys

'Unless the seed falls to the ground and dies, it will remain only one seed, but if it dies, it will produce many seeds – Heartbeat needs to die!'

At various points throughout our lives, God has asked us to put something to death so that He could raise it back to life perhaps in a different form. Death is never easy but as we trust God to take us through the darkness we will discover that what we move into is an even more fruitful place.

Ray and I had always said that if God told us to put Heartbeat to death then we would do it. We knew God had put the vision of a music and mission team into our hearts and if God said that the time for Heartbeat's ministry was over, then we would not want it to continue. There is a huge difference, though, in saying that statement and actually obeying God and putting it into practice. In 1990 Heartbeat had been working in ministry for almost ten years. In that time we had literally seen thousands of people come to know the Lord and thousands of people healed from various illnesses. We had seen thousands of Christians re-dedicate their lives to Christ. Our sphere of influence had moved from a national one to an international one. We had had many missions and events in mainland Europe and many invitations to travel in the States. Our albums were being sold all over the world. One of the tracks from our *The Winner* album had reached number three in the American Christian Music charts. We were receiving letters from people as far away as Australia telling us they loved our music and the message we brought. Just when we seemed to be at our most 'successful', we felt God speak to us and tell us that it was time for Heartbeat to die.

We asked Ken McGreavy if he would pray with us that if God was asking us to put Heartbeat to death, He would make that very clear and plain. Just after that, Ray went to a meeting where Gerald Coates was speaking. Afterwards Gerald took Ray aside and told him that a number of weeks previously he had felt a burden to pray for Ray and myself. He mentioned this to Trish Richards, whom Gerald knew often heard prophetic words from God for others, and asked her if she had received anything from God for Heartbeat. She said she hadn't but the very next morning she woke up with a dream, which she felt was for us. As Gerald explained the dream to Ray, it was not hard to see that God was talking about Heartbeat dying and that we would be moving from our base in Malmesbury.

A few weeks later, we met Lynn Green from Youth with a Mission at a mission we were doing in Swindon. At that event, Lynn gave Ray and me a word from God about Heartbeat. He felt God was saying that 'unless the seed falls to the ground and dies, it would remain only one seed, but if it dies, it would produce many seeds' (John 12:24). I can still remember Lynn telling us that day, 'Ray, Nancy, I feel God is telling you that Heartbeat should die, and if you obey God in this, you will be much more effective in the future.'

We took these words back to God and continued to ask Him for wisdom as to what to do. When we next saw Ken, he too told us he felt the time was right for Heartbeat to finish. At that point we then shared with the others in Heartbeat the words we had received from God. As you can imagine this was a huge shock to everyone, but we stressed that even if Heartbeat closed down, that did not mean that they needed to leave ngm. We assured all of them that there would always be a place for them if they wanted to walk into the future with us. However, we realised from the word that Trish Richards had given us, that some 'arrows' would fly in other directions and it was right for some to move on to other ministries. Although there was much sadness at Heartbeat's ministry finishing, as we continued to pray it became obvious that this was what God was calling us to do.

We decided that Heartbeat would close in September 1991. That last year was so difficult as we walked through a minefield of emotions within the team. However, we could not deny that God had spoken and therefore despite the difficulties we knew it would be disobedient to keep the ministry going. Our last concert was held at the De Montfort Hall in Leicester. As I looked out on the audience that night before going on stage, tears were pouring down my face. The 2,200-seat hall was packed with people, many of whom had come to know the Lord through the work of Heartbeat. I was remembering that when Ray and I started Heartbeat in 1981, we could hardly get an audience of one to come and listen to us. Here we were ten years later in a huge venue celebrating all that God had done through us. God had indeed been faithful.

During 1991, there were around sixteen people in ngm. Eight of those who had been in Heartbeat left in the September when we closed Heartbeat down. Shortly thereafter, we moved from Malmesbury to Thornbury in Bristol where God has blessed and increased our work. At the time of writing this book, we now have approximately 120 people working in ngm. We have eleven teams working in eight locations. As the one seed died, God produced many seeds. It has also been great to see how God has led and blessed the others who left Heartbeat. It is so important to obey God despite how difficult that is at times. However, if we obey, our faith will increase and develop.

Do remember that God knows the end from the beginning. All He requires of us is to take His hand and trust Him to lead us through the minefields along the way. For those of you who are parents of young children you will identify with the wonderful feeling of a child's small hand in yours. When a child is insecure, fearful or just cautious, they will often come and take your hand. They know you will protect and help them to deal with whatever is bothering them. They simply put their faith in you and in the love you have for them. God wants us to come as little children and put our hands into His, knowing that He loves us much more than we could ever love our children. If we listen, are obedient, and put our trust in Him, He will lead us through each problem or 'death' into the many fantastic new areas He has for us.

Exercises for your faith muscles

▶ Read Matthew 18:3. What does it mean to become like a little child? How does this relate to our faith?

▶ Read 2 Corinthians 4:7–11. What does it mean to die to selfish desires? How does the truth in these verses affect our faith and life in God? How can you apply these verses more in your own life?

▶ Read 1 Samuel 15.
  1. What does this chapter teach us about obedience to God?
  2. Saul had not fully obeyed the Lord's instructions (1 Samuel 15:21–22) and tried to justify his disobedience. Examine your own heart and see if there have been times when you have done or have been tempted to do the same.
  3. Meditate on 1 Samuel 15:22 and write down/discuss what you receive from God through this verse.

▶ Memorise James 1:22:

> 'Do not merely listen to the word, and so deceive yourselves. Do what it says.'

Chapter 12

Salvation Faith

'Hugh wouldn't you like to become a Christian?'

When I became a Christian at the young age of six years, God planted a deep desire within me to tell others about Him. I couldn't wait to tell everyone that Jesus was alive and that He could change our lives. I was desperate to know Jesus for myself, so one day I asked my Dad if I could give my life to God. Dad looked down at his little daughter and must have wondered if I really knew what I was doing. Giving your life to Jesus is not something you should do lightly, but something that should be a life commitment. My Dad wondered if I really understood what I was doing, and then very kindly suggested that I wait until I was a little older. I accepted his advice, but God had other ideas.

One Sunday evening, when my Mum and two of her friends were at church, God spoke so clearly to me and changed my life forever. My Dad was putting my little three-year-old brother, Jack, to bed. I was in the lounge, not thinking about anything to do with God or Christianity, when something strange happened to me. I was standing with my back to the fire in front of our couch, when I lost the power to stand and fell to my knees. I tried to push myself up by using the couch but I couldn't. I laid my head down on the couch to rest for a little

115

while before trying again. I couldn't understand what was happening to me. Why had I lost the power in my legs?

I decided to try again, but when I tried to lift my head, I discovered I couldn't lift it from the couch. It was as if a big hand had been placed over the back of my legs and a big hand over the back of my neck. As I heard the voice of God gently call my name, I suddenly realised that I was in a praying position. This was the way my Mum and Dad had taught me to pray each night, kneeling before my bed. I knew God was speaking to me and I knew He wanted me to become a Christian, but I didn't know what to say. My Mum and Dad had always spoken my prayers for me and I had just repeated what they had said. So I said my first real prayer, which was, 'Dear God, I'll tell my Daddy.' Immediately I uttered those words the pressure lifted and I was able to lift my head and stand again. A few seconds later my Father entered the room and I excitedly told him of my experience of God. He immediately prayed with me and that evening I asked the Creator of the Universe – the only true God – into my life.

I had always been brought up to know that God was real, but that night I experienced Him for myself. My little heart was so full it almost burst with excitement. God was real and He had come to live in my heart. I knew my life's destiny from that moment on was to tell others about the amazing God who had made Himself known to me.

When my Mum and her friends, Dawn and Hugh, came back from church, I could not wait to tell them what I had experienced. Even although I had become a Christian, my Dad still said I had to go to bed, but sleep that night was far from me. When the front door opened and my Mum arrived home, I ran to the top of our stairs and shouted to her to come up quickly. I think she thought the house was on fire when she and her friends came bounding up the stairs. However, when they arrived in my bedroom the only thing that was on fire was my heart. I was bouncing up and down on my bed with sheer joy. I told them I had become a Christian and immediately challenged Hugh to give his life to the Lord. Dawn had become a Christian a number of weeks previously, but Hugh had not done so. As I asked him if he wanted to give his life to Jesus, he had to leave the room as tears started to pour down his face.

I decided from that moment on that Hugh was my first prayer target. Now I wouldn't recommend this as the best evangelistic tool to help you in your outreach, but what I put into effect made a huge difference in Hugh's life. I decided that as well as pray for Hugh, I would also sit beside him each Sunday night when we went to church. We attended a Brethren assembly and on each Sunday evening they would have what I called a 'hell fire' gospel message. The preacher would always challenge the audience by pointing his finger at them and saying something like, 'If you leave this place tonight not knowing Christ and get run over by a bus, do you know you are going to hell?' I would make sure that Hugh would understand that the preacher was talking to him by putting my elbow into his ribs. As the preacher emphasised this point several times in one preach, Hugh must have been black and blue by the end of the service. He survived two weeks of me digging him in the ribs, before giving his life to the Lord. Praise God, I had my first convert.

As I said before, I wouldn't recommend this type of evangelistic approach; however, targeting people in prayer is essential if you want to see them give their lives to God. It is so important to bring them to God in prayer and to pray for them each day or as often as you can. Then, as you are praying for them, combine your prayers with your faith and begin to see God move in their situations.

My next target was my little brother, Jack. He was only three when I became a Christian but every night before he went to sleep, I preached to him. As we shared the same bedroom, he got a hell fire message each night. It must have scared the living daylights out of him! I told him that my Mum and Dad were going to heaven and so were my two older brothers, Jim and Tom, and now so was I. However, he would not be able to go to heaven because he had not yet given his life to Jesus. I asked him again and again, would he not like to give his heart to the Lord? Just after he reached the age of four, a few months since I became a Christian, he asked Mum if he could pray and ask Jesus to come into his life and give him the assurance of going to heaven too.

It was shortly after that time that my cousin, Ann, came to stay at our house for a number of weeks. As I shared a room with her, I decided to ask God to bring my cousin into a living relationship with Him. I again targeted her in prayer and prayed that I would see the day that Ann would give her life to the Lord. After a number of nights of my preaching, she too gave her life to the Lord Jesus. It didn't take long before there were quite a number of people saved through combining my simple faith with my eager prayers.

Can I encourage you to target your friends for Christ? Pray for them, fast for them, ask God to give you opportunities to speak out for Him. Pray within your faith. What can you envisage God doing? Ask God to give you opportunities to tell them about Him. You will find that when you combine your faith with prayer, amazing things will happen.

Some of you might have been praying for your friends for some time and yet have not seen the breakthrough that you have been longing for. Can I encourage you to keep going even if you do not see with your human eyes the progress you have been longing for? Ask God to open your spiritual eyes and begin to see His plan.

When I started secondary school I was keen to see my friends become Christians. I prayed for an opportunity to share with my best friend that I was a Christian. One Monday morning while walking to school, she suddenly asked me what I had done the previous day. I took a deep breath and told her I went to church. To my utter surprise she seemed very interested. She asked questions like 'Why do you go to church?' It was exciting to answer her questions even although she told me that she was an atheist. When we arrived at school I was riding high in faith, when suddenly I was brought back to earth with a huge bump. My friend couldn't wait to tell everyone 'Hey everyone, listen to this! You will never believe this, but Nancy believes in

God!' The sarcasm in her voice was not hard to miss. I wanted the ground to open up and for me to disappear into it. My best friend was making me feel a fool.

However, from that one comment, a huge discussion ensued about whether people believed in God or not. Everyone wanted to know why I had put my faith in a God I couldn't see. After a number of weeks, one of the girls who had been in that discussion gave her life to Jesus. I was determined, however, not to give up on my best friend and so although I could see no way that she would become a Christian, I still prayed for her and asked God to impact her life. I didn't have much faith because she had been so vocally against what I had said, but I asked God to perform a miracle nonetheless.

I invited her to come to church with me and to my surprise she accepted, even though she had to wear a hat! In my church all the females had to wear head coverings and none of them were allowed to speak in public. As we sat there with our huge hats on that would have looked great at Ascot, but I am sure looked ridiculous on us, she would listen to what the preacher had to say. If she disagreed with him, which happened to be quite often, she would shout out in the meeting 'No' or 'That's not true'. It was something that had never happened in our Brethren meetings before. You could see the surprised and embarrassed look on everyone's faces – including mine. However, after a number of months of her attending our church and other Christian meetings, she asked my Mum if she could speak to her privately. I couldn't understand why she would want to speak to my Mum, but about 15 minutes later she told me the news that she had given her life to the Lord. I could not have seen that happen with my natural eyes as she had been so negative about Christianity, but God can break through any barriers and speak even to the hardest of hearts.

Just recently I met a lady at one of my Spiritual Health Conferences who later wrote to me to tell me this amazing story. She had prayed in faith for her husband for thirty years. She loved him so much and did not want him to go to a Christless eternity. He was a man who had lived all his life in good health when suddenly he had a heart attack and died. However, in the last few seconds of his life, he gave his life to Christ. Eileen's faith-filled prayers had not been in vain. When I heard this story I felt quickened in my spirit to write to Eileen and say 'well done'. I am sure that there were many times during those thirty years when Eileen must have questioned whether her prayers were being heard, never mind being answered. The temptation to give up must have been huge and yet as she had faithfully prayed over the years, God had not only heard her prayer, but also remembered them as a sweet smell before Him. Just at the right time He answered her prayers and took Dennis, her husband, into eternity to be with Him forever. Her faith-filled prayers were answered.

I was attending an event a number of years ago in London when I heard a story about a young girl who was so keen to share her faith with others that she knocked on a number of doors each night on her way home from school. When the person inside answered her persistent knocking, she would tell them about her faith in Jesus and challenge them to become Christians. The remarkable thing about this was that she lived in a Buddhist country, but she did not let that stop her. She combined her faith with action and asked God to lead her to the right doors. One day she encountered a young seventeen-year-old lad who was dying from tuberculosis. As she told him about her faith in God, he told her that he was not interested in Christianity. She was not put off, however, as she knew that if he did not give his life to God, in a year or so he would die and go to a lost eternity. She determined within herself to go back to this particular house each day. Even though this young lad rejected her again and again, she continued to go back.

On the Friday after she had visited his house each day that week, he got very angry with her and told her quite clearly not to return. Instead of giving up she immediately sank to her knees and started to pray with tears running down her face for this teenager's life. He immediately felt compassion for her and said 'Please don't cry – I will become a Christian just for you.'

She immediately said, 'If you are serious about this then, please take this Bible and promise me you will read it.' He said he would and during the coming weeks he began to read the New Testament she had given him. During the reading of that Bible he not only gave his life to God but he was also actively praying and claiming his healing. God not only gave him assurance of eternity with Him, but also healed him completely to the utter amazement of his family. That man went on to become the pastor of the largest church in the world. His name is Pastor Paul Yongi Cho. That young girl persisted in her faith-filled prayers and God honoured her for doing so by answering those prayers.

Can I encourage you to keep on praying? Don't give up. Even if it takes many years to see the answers to your prayers, please don't give up. God is listening and He longs to bring your friend or family member to Himself much more than even you do. Keep on going despite not seeing with your human eyes the answers to your prayers. Remember what the Bible says:

'The one who calls you is faithful and he will do it.'
(1 Thessalonians 5:24)

Exercises for your faith muscles

▶ Read Matthew 15:21–28. What can we learn from these verses about faith?

▶ Name or write down the person or people you are praying for. Start to pray for them in relation to your faith. Do not pray for them to break down in tears and urgently want God in their lives if that is not within your faith. Instead ask yourself a question – what can I believe God to do in my friend(s) at this moment in time? For example, can you believe God for a good conversation with them? Pray for what lies within your faith and then when you see God answer that, move onto the next step you can believe God for.

As you pray into each step make sure you look out for the opportunities God puts in your way. Keep listening, obeying, trusting and moving with God in your journey of faith.

► Meditate on 1 Thessalonians 5:24. Write down/discuss what God says through this verse.

► Memorise Philemon 6:

'I pray that you may be active in sharing your faith, so that you will have a full understanding of every good thing we have in Christ.'

Chapter 13

Shield of Faith

'I need to run some tests, but I think you may have rheumatoid arthritis.'

As I sat in the doctor's surgery I felt tension rise in my being. I could not believe what I was hearing. Could I possibly have rheumatoid arthritis? Surely not! I had just given birth a few months earlier to my first son, Daniel. He was a great little boy who brought such a lot of joy into our lives. However, a number of months after the birth I started to feel such pain in my joints. When I woke each morning I could hardly move any of my joints, they were so sore and continued to be like that until I pushed through the pain threshold and moved my fingers, hands, arms, legs etc. Once I got going, the pain disappeared until I sat in one place for any length of time – then the pain would come back and I would have to go through the whole process again. I felt as if I had aged overnight and become an old woman.

The doctor sent me to a specialist who examined me and took some blood tests. During this time, Ray and I and the whole of ngm were praying for God to somehow intervene and heal me. Nothing seemed to happen and I continued to move in pain. When I next visited the doctor he told me, much to my relief, that I did not have rheumatoid arthritis. However, the doctor was bewildered as to what I did have. He took more tests but each one came back negative.

I could not understand what was happening to me. Why was God not answering my prayers for healing? I continued to plead before God and ask Him to take this illness from me but no healing appeared. One day I heard God plainly say to me, 'Ask the team to pray for you once more and as you do, I will heal you.' I felt embarrassed to ask the team to pray again for me, but I knew God had spoken and so I laid aside my embarrassment and said, 'I am really sorry guys, but would you pray for me just once more. I felt God say that if you prayed for me today, He would heal me.' As the team started to pray there was nothing to suggest that this prayer meeting was any different to the others. However, after a few minutes our keyboard player, Dave Bankhead, had a specific word of knowledge. He felt someone close to me had spoken words against me and that those words had acted like a curse in my life. He felt that if we broke the words then my healing would come. As he prayed for me that morning I knew God had healed me. I felt set free, even though I could not tell whether I was physically healed or not. However, the next morning when I got up, there was no pain! God had completely healed me.

About a week later, after Ray and I had travelled to Bath to go shopping, I felt the pain come back. I was stiff again getting out of the car. I knew in my spirit that if I accepted this illness back again, then my healing would disappear. I felt annoyed at the enemy for trying to put this illness back on me. I told Ray, 'I am just not accepting this. Would you stand with me and pray that this illness would go in the name of Jesus?' Ray and I both then prayed and rebuked the enemy. Each time I felt the stiffness come back I would reject it and speak out that I wasn't having this illness back again. By the end of my shopping trip, the pain had disappeared, never to return.

We often do not realise how much power there is in the spoken word. In Genesis when God *spoke*, there was so much power in those words that our world was created. In the New

Testament when Jesus *spoke*, amazing miracles happened: blind eyes were able to see, deaf ears were opened, new hands were created and the dead were raised. When Jesus cursed a fig tree, it withered and died. There is much power in the spoken word. Jesus said to His disciples,

> *'I tell you the truth, if you have faith as small as a mustard seed, you can say to this mountain, "Move from here to there" and it will move. Nothing will be impossible for you.'*
>
> (Matthew 17:20)

We need to be careful to use our words to build others up rather than tear them down. We should also be aware that we can use our faith, however small it is, to rebuke the enemy and see him flee. I know if Ray and I had not stood against the enemy that day while I was in Bath, my illness would have come back, but it was as I *spoke* against the illness and cursed it in the name of Jesus, that it had to wither and die.

A number of years ago, whilst on mission in Portsmouth, Ray and I encountered demonic activity. I woke up in the middle of the night feeling that the enemy was in our room. As fear tugged at my heart, I heard a sound from Ray as if he was choking. Ray then shouted out the name of Jesus and suddenly the demonic presence was gone. Ray was then able to tell me that he had woken up with what felt like hands around his neck. He had felt as though he was being strangled, until he managed to shout out the name of Jesus. We so often forget what power there is in the name of Jesus.

Our mission in Portsmouth continued with great results. We visited one particular school where we realised that the Religious Education teacher did not want us in the school. Although it was obvious to us that she did not want us in her classes, the headmaster had warmly invited us to sing and speak to all the pupils, and he brought each year group into the assembly hall so that they would have a chance to hear us. At the end of the week we held an event where we invited the pupils to come along to a concert with Heartbeat where they had an opportunity to become Christians. We normally held the end-of-the-week-concert in another venue but the organisers of the mission had decided to hire the school for this particular evening event. That night the hall was packed and many responded to say they wanted to give their lives to Jesus. We went back to our hosts' houses rejoicing at all that God had done.

However, the next morning it was as if 'all hell' had been let loose. Ray got a phone call from one of the organisers to say that he and the organiser were being summonsed to the headmaster's study. When Ray walked into the room he said it was like walking into 'the lions' den'. The headmaster had received so many complaints about the previous night and wanted to find out what had happened. In this meeting there was a governor of the school, the RE teacher, a pupil and a parent, and for the next hour or so Ray and Graham the organiser were shouted at as they accused us of many things.

They told the headmaster that we had 'bouncers' who controlled the audience. In reality we had no bouncers, only a few older Christians who were helping to make sure the event went well. They said that Ray had preached a message that if people did not give their lives to Jesus that night, then they would go to hell and would endure a long slow painful death. In reality Ray did not mention hell once and obviously did not say they would experience a long slow painful death. They then said we had locked those who had responded in a room where we would not let them out unless they gave us their names and addresses. In reality all we had done was to ask those who responded to go into an unlocked room where the counsellors could pray for them. And after they had become Christians we asked if we could have their names and address so that we could give them to the local church. This meant that the local church could invite them to further activities that would be organised for them. They also gave an example of two sisters who attended the event. One of them gave her life to Jesus and went home thrilled at what God had done in her life, the other did not respond to God and went home in tears with the conviction of God on her. They could not understand why both sisters who had attended the same event could come away with completely different experiences. Although we explained all these situations to them they would not stop shouting and accusing us. The headmaster said he would look into this matter but that from now on all the schools in Hampshire would close their doors to the work of Heartbeat.

As we prayed with the church later that evening we realised that God had given us a word at the beginning of the week:

'See, I have placed before you an open door ...'
(Revelation 3:8)

As we prayed we spoke out those words and trusted that somehow God would open the doors that the enemy had shut.

In the next few weeks many letters started appearing in the local press about what had 'supposedly' happened that night. People from the local church then responded by writing and saying, 'Actually, I was there and this is what really happened; this is what Ray said.' They then took the opportunity of sharing the story of how they had become Christians. Many testimonies of how people had become Christians appeared in the local paper. We continued to pray that God would somehow reverse the decision made to close the doors of these schools to the work of Heartbeat. Eventually, months later, Ray and Graham were again asked to go to the headmaster's study. This time only the headmaster was present. He said, 'I have asked you to come here today so that I can apologise to you both. I have looked into this matter thoroughly and cannot back up any of the accusations that were thrust at you. I have discovered that there is no truth in any of the accusations and all I can say is that there must have been "a certain ethos" around that evening.' He then asked Ray and Graham what we would like him to do. We asked him to clear Heartbeat's name and open the doors to the schools in Hampshire again. The headmaster agreed and we also asked that Graham, the organiser of the event, be in charge of who came into the school to teach Religious Education. As we trusted and spoke out victory throughout those months, as we put our faith into action and believed Him, God brought a miracle into place.

The doors seemed so firmly closed and yet God had spoken that the doors would open. They were indeed opened wide. You might be looking at your 'mountain' and thinking there is no way you can stand against the enemy in this one. Do remember that you are not on your own, God is with you and if God is for you, who can stand against you? (Romans 8:31). If God has spoken then believe His word and even if Satan sets himself up against you, he will not prevail. Speak out God's words; trust in Him and the gates of hell will fall at your feet.

Exercises for your faith muscles

▶ Think through the words you speak each day. Are they helpful and kind? Do they produce faith in you and in others or do they pull both yourself and others down?

▶ Listen to or read from my meditation CD *Peace like a River*, track 5 (see back of book for details). Write down what God says to you. Spend some time praying about the words of your mouth.

Forest Fire
I want you to come with me on a journey, a journey that will take you to a place of peace and rest and will bring well-being to your soul.

Prepare yourself by making sure you are lying or sitting in a comfortable position. Breathe in deeply and expel the air slowly. As you let the air out, speak to your inner being and say the word 'relax'. Breathe in and relax. Breathe in and relax.

Now close your eyes and begin to see with the eyes of your heart. In your imagination, begin to see a huge forest of strong and well-developed trees. You long to go and explore all the ancient paths, which criss-cross throughout this forest, but before you can do so you notice a woman walking by. As you watch her, she lights up a cigarette and carelessly throws away the match. Unknown to her that small match is still burning and because the forest is so dry it isn't long before a fire starts. Before you can shout for help the small fire grows and grows and suddenly is out of control. You stand back in horror as the flames cause total destruction. Minutes before, you were looking at creativity and beauty at its highest level, now all you can see is a huge ball of fire as it devours everything in sight. Your heart is filled with sadness at the destruction around you.

The picture then changes. Begin to see yourself looking at the forest long after the fire has been put out. You walk through the charred and black remains, disturbed in your spirit about the waste of life. All the trees and their beauty have been burned and destroyed. All around you is death and destruction. As you stand appalled at the waste of life you notice at various points in the soil that someone has come and planted new young trees alongside the dead ones. Someone has planted shrubs and flowers in the midst of decay. Already these young trees are beginning to grow and these plants are beginning to take root. Your heart is suddenly revived as you see that out of a desolate situation, life is prevailing. You rejoice in the life you see and know that if you were to come back to this land many years from now the scene would once again be teeming with life.

In the Bible it says, *'the tongue is a small part of the body, but it makes great boasts'* (James 3:5). Consider what a great forest is set on fire by a small spark. The tongue can be that small spark bringing destruction and corruption to all around.

At various points in our lives, careless words can be like a tiny spark of destruction thrown into your heart. Some words can cause a huge fire deep within you and may even leave you feeling destroyed. However, just as that forest can be renewed and refreshed so can your heart, spirit, soul and body be made new again. Speak to your spirit and plant wise and healing words within you. Plant words such as 'I am not a mistake.' 'I am loved.' 'I am special.' 'There is nothing I cannot do.' 'There is no one quite like me.' Continue to plant positive words within you each day and soon you will see them taking root. Plant good, wise and healing words and so like that forest, you will begin to feel strong and whole again.

An old proverb says, 'Words can kill. Words give life. They are either poison or fruit – you choose.'

(Nancy Goudie, ngm/SGO Publishing 2002)

▶ Meditate on Philippians 2:9–11. Write down/discuss what God says through this meditation.

▶ Memorise Matthew 17:20:

'I tell you the truth, if you have faith as small as a mustard seed, you can say to this mountain, "Move from here to there" and it will move. Nothing will be impossible for you.'

Chapter 14

Faith Listens

'Nancy, I believe God has told me there is someone in the audience tonight who has leprosy and if I pray for them God is going to heal them.' My response was 'Leprosy! Ray, this is England not Africa. Surely no one in England has leprosy!'

As I have travelled, I have met many people who tell me they find it difficult to hear God speak to them. They are amazed at stories where God has spoken so clearly and wish they could have a more intimate relationship with Jesus. The good news is that God loves to speak to His children and all He requires from us is that we have ears that are open and willing to hear. If you find it difficult to hear from God then let me list a few pointers that could be helpful.

Firstly, we must exercise our faith and believe that God exists and wants to communicate with us. This seems so obvious and yet some people have already pre-conditioned themselves to believe that God does not want to communicate with them. Then secondly, we need to open our ears and tune in to His voice. Hearing from God is like tuning into a radio station. When you try and tune into a certain radio station it takes time and effort to pass all the sounds and signals you hear en route and find the exact radio programme you desire. Similarly, if we want to hear from God, then we need to fine-tune ourselves to hear His voice and not all the other noises that are going on in our heads. Fine-tuning comes through reading His written

Word, through meditating on Scripture and through prayer. There are many ways that God can speak to us: through the Bible, visions or pictures, dreams, the preaching or teaching of the Word, through other people, prophetic words or through a still small voice. Learn to trust what you hear and, as I have said earlier, don't be afraid to share what you have received with someone else, perhaps someone who is further along the road with God than you. As you grow in love for God and develop greater intimacy with God, He will reveal more of His heart for you and for the people around you.

I remember being on mission in Oxfordshire many years ago when God said to me that in the audience that night there would be a boy who was a habitual stealer. He could not stop stealing whether it was from his friends or from others around him. I felt God say that if he would come to God that night and give his life to Him, then God would break the bondage he was in and free him from his habit of stealing.

That night, I stood and shared what I had received from God. What happened was both surprising and amazing! Most of the audience came from one school that we had been working in during the week and therefore most of the people there knew one another. When I said I believed there was someone in the audience who could not stop stealing whether it was from his friends, family or whoever, all the audience turned round and pointed to this one boy saying 'It's him, it's him!' That night that young guy gave his life to the Lord Jesus; all because I trusted what God had given me to say.

I remember another time in Blackburn where we were holding an evangelistic event. We had been in the schools in the area and had prayed for the Lord to fill the main hall in Blackburn with 'unchurched' people. We had an amazing time where God brought hundreds of people to the event, and many of those people gave their lives to Jesus. One night, Ray felt he had received a word of knowledge from God that there would be someone in the audience that night with leprosy. When he shared it with me, I said the obvious. 'Ray, are you sure? This is England not Africa. Surely there is no one in this country with leprosy!' He said, 'I know, that's why I am bouncing it off you – what do you think I should do?' I looked into his eyes and said 'If you believe it is of God, then go for it, Ray.' You see I knew my husband often heard from God very clearly. As we prayed about it with Heartbeat just before going on stage I remember someone in the team saying, 'Can you not just say that there is someone here with a skin disorder rather than say leprosy?' Ray said, ' No, God has definitely said leprosy.'

So that night, my brave husband put his trust and faith in God and in His word. He stood at the front of the stage and clearly said that God had spoken to him earlier and told him that there would be someone in the audience that night with leprosy and that if they reached out to God, He was going to heal them. That night, two people were healed from leprosy. They had just flown in from another country and both of them had leprosy. When we step out in faith and believe God, He will be faithful to His word.

At another of our events God spoke to me and told me that a girl in the audience would be suffering from tonsillitis and that if we prayed for her she would be healed. I also felt that we should pray that the tonsillitis would not be so bad that the person would be unable to attend. At the end of the event, a girl approached Ray and said she had tonsillitis and nearly didn't come because it had been so bad. But during the afternoon (when we had been praying) it got slightly better so she came. Praise God that as we prayed for her, her headache disappeared and her glands went back to normal. If we hadn't trusted God and obeyed what He had said, this girl may not have been healed.

God is looking for people who will not only listen to what He is saying but will also trust Him and do what He says. Noah was someone who trusted God despite the circumstances. Noah lived in a day when most of the people around him did not listen or obey God, but Noah was different. As it says in Genesis,

'Noah was a righteous man, blameless among the people of his time, and he walked with God.' (Genesis 6:9)

God spoke to Noah and told him that He was going to destroy the earth because of all the evil that was happening. He gave Noah clear instructions to build an ark in which he was to place not only himself, his wife, his sons and his sons' wives, but also two of each kind of animal on the earth. Can you imagine getting a word from God like that? 'Build a *what*, God? An ark? What's an ark? What would I want with a boat in the middle of the desert miles from the sea? Rain, Lord? What is rain?' Until then, God had not brought rain on the earth and therefore Noah would not have understood what rain was. 'You are going to bring rain? Thousands of little droplets of water which will fall from the sky on this earth so that the whole earth will be flooded?' It seems unbelievable doesn't it?

Nonetheless, Noah trusted God even though many people would have laughed at him and ridiculed him as he built his boat. 'Are you drunk, Noah? Are you mad? What on earth are you building a massively huge boat for? We are miles from the sea.' Yet despite the opposition to the word of the Lord, he kept building and obeying what God had said. It was only as he obeyed and kept his eyes on God that he and his family were saved from the terrible flood that wiped out all known civilisation.

I heard a story a few years back about a man called Smith Wigglesworth. He was a man whose life story constantly inspires me and challenges me in my walk with God. What thrills me the most about Smith Wigglesworth is that he was an ordinary man, a plumber from Bradford, yet God used him in extraordinary ways. If you read any of the books written about Smith Wigglesworth you will discover that he had no formal education, in fact he could not read or write until he was married. Before God called him to be a preacher he was the most reluctant preacher you could ever meet. He was very happy just to put out the chairs at the mission where his wife was preaching and after the appeal to pray for the many who responded. He had no ambition to preach at all and yet God used him in incredible ways to reach others. As a preacher he saw thousands give their lives to Christ and thousands healed through the power of God. The one thing that truly marked out Smith Wigglesworth was his intimacy with God and his walk and life of faith.

When I was preaching in Wells a few years ago, I met a lady who had been a friend of Smith Wigglesworth when he was alive and she told me this story. Smith Wigglesworth was walking down a road one day, when God spoke to him and said, 'Smith, do you see the door of that house over there?' When Smith Wigglesworth said yes, God then said, 'I want you to go to that door and lift up the letterbox and shout through the letterbox that I am real and that I love the world.' Smith Wigglesworth was used to God telling him to do strange things but this was a new one for him. His response to God was probably the same as ours would have been if God had asked us to do that. 'God I'm sorry, I just cannot do that.' However, God insisted, 'I want you to go and lift up that letterbox and shout through it that I am real and that I love the world.' As Smith Wigglesworth walked passed the door, he argued with God and said, 'I'm sorry Lord I just cannot do that!'

I have much sympathy for Smith Wigglesworth. Can you imagine God asking you to do that? You can understand why he kept on walking along the road. However, the moment he walked past the door, the conviction of God fell on him and he said 'Okay God, I will do it.' You see Smith Wigglesworth was a man who had said to God many years before that he would always do what God had told him to do, no matter how crazy it might seem to him at the time. He had promised God that he would be obedient. So he walked back to the house, opened up the letterbox and shouted in his huge booming voice,

> 'For God so loved the world that he gave his one and only Son, that whoever believes in him shall not perish but have eternal life.' (John 3:16)

He then closed the letterbox and started walking down the road.

A few minutes later, the door of the house opened and a man came running out. He looked up and down the road. There was only one person in sight and that was Smith Wigglesworth so he ran after him. As he approached Smith he said, 'Excuse me, but did you just happen to shout through my letterbox?' When Smith Wigglesworth affirmed that this was so the man then said, 'Let me tell you my story. I was in that house ready to commit suicide. I was standing on a box with a rope around my neck. I had just said to myself, "There is no one in this world that cares whether I live or die. There is no one who loves me." I was just about to kick the box away when a big booming voice shouted through my letterbox.' He asked, 'Tell me, is it true? Does God love me?' Smith Wigglesworth had the amazing opportunity of leading that man to Jesus all because he had trusted God's voice and obeyed what seemed God's crazy instructions.

It is important that each of us not only learns to hear and trust what God says to us but also obeys what He has asked us to do. Many miracles lie dormant because we don't put our faith into action and obey God.

Just recently I heard an amazing story from a lady who approached me at a festival where I was preaching. She told me that she had been at one of my spiritual health days many years previously where God had spoken to her so clearly. She heard God ask her to buy one of my meditation CDs and take it to her brother who was in a mental home at the time and play it to him. I am sure the thought of taking one of my meditation CDs to her brother in a mental institute must have seemed quite daunting. However, that day she bought one of my recordings and played it to her brother. When she did so, her brother was instantaneously healed. The only reason her brother was healed was because that lady not only opened her ears and listened to the voice of God, but also because she was prepared to obey what God had said, no matter how bizarre it sounded.

Today, let's tell God our ears are open to His voice. Let's believe what God says to us and then let's do what He says. If we live in submission to God, obeying what He tells us, we will see miracles happen.

Exercises for your faith muscles

▶ Think through/discuss reasons why you may find it difficult at times to hear God's voice. Bring each reason to God in prayer and ask Him to show you how to hear His voice more clearly.

▶ Think through/discuss the step that needs to be taken to move from hearing God to obeying God. Be honest! How difficult/easy do you find this?

▶ Meditate on Hebrews 11:6: *'Without faith it is impossible to please God.'* Write down/discuss what you receive from God through this meditation. Finish by examining your lifestyle – are there areas of your life where you are not displaying faith? Pray and spend time handing over to God any area where you are not displaying faith.

▶ Memorise Hebrews 11:6:

'Without faith it is impossible to please God.'

Chapter 15

Faith Acts

'Well, this should be interesting! How are you going to get round this one, Lord?'

It was 1992 and we were in the process of moving from Malmesbury to Thornbury near Bristol. When we had received the word from God about Heartbeat finishing, part of that word was that we would move from Malmesbury to somewhere a short distance away. After much prayer and discussion we felt that we should move to be with our friends from Bristol Christian Fellowship, which was only a half an hour's journey away. We had worked with this church many times throughout the years as we had done missions with them in the area and had built up some very strong friendships with a number of them and with the leaders there. We had discovered through the years that they were a very loving, generous church, which was borne out when we physically moved to Thornbury. One couple allowed us to stay in their home for a month before we found a rented house. Another couple gave us a brand new school uniform for Daniel just before he started his first day at school. When we eventually did buy a home in Thornbury, many from the church came and helped decorate the house for us. Their sacrificial help was such a blessing to us.

Although Ray and I had sold our home and moved, we still had to travel back to Malmesbury as our offices and studio were there. We knew this could not continue and so we began to ask God where we should 'house' our offices and have our base. Each day in our travels to Malmesbury we passed by a manor house called 'The Ridge', which was partly owned by the Bristol Christian Fellowship. We knew the church only used the house occasionally for church meetings and so we began to pray whether this could be the right place for us to have our offices and base. The more we prayed the more convinced we became that this was indeed the right place for us. It wasn't in Thornbury itself but it was only six miles away, very near the M4/M5 junction.

We approached the elders to ask if it was possible for us to have a couple of the bedrooms as offices. Eventually they invited us to attend one of their elders' meetings, which was held in the building in question. After Ray outlined exactly what we were asking and what it would mean, the elders then began to discuss the possibility. We knew the elders wanted to help us if they could, but as the conversation progressed it was obvious due to concerns over planning permission that the answer was going to be no. I remember inwardly talking to the Lord saying, 'Lord, I am convinced you want us to have this place as our offices, so it is going to be interesting to find out how you will change their minds.'

As the discussion came to a close and the elders said, 'Sorry, Ray and Nancy, I don't really think it is going to be possible,' suddenly one elder, who had remained silent throughout the whole discussion, made a comment that totally changed the situation. With that one comment, the answer now was that if we could get planning permission for change of use, then the elders would allow us to have our offices there.

We went back to the team with renewed vigour to pray and fast, as it seemed unlikely that the planning permission for change of use would be granted. As you can imagine, it takes some time for planning permission to be given and during that time we had several people say to us, 'It is so sad that you will not be able to use The Ridge as your base.' When we said that we were praying and believing that we would be able to use it, they were surprised, as they did not think there was any way we would get the permission we needed.

We kept going back and asking God if we had indeed heard from Him that He would bring us a positive word from the planning department. There was great rejoicing when we received a phone call from one of the elders who told us that the planning permission had been granted. The church allowed us to rent two of the bedrooms and the landing and we shared the kitchen and upstairs lounge with them. They also allowed us to house our studios in one of their buildings in the centre of Bristol at no cost, but that is another story.

We have discovered through the years that faith is always active. When we embark upon any faith venture it is not a matter of 'looking and observing' – God wants us to be actively involved.

When Daniel was reading the Scriptures it says he discovered that God had promised through the prophet Jeremiah that the desolation of Jerusalem would last seventy years (Daniel 9; Jeremiah 25:11–12). Now Daniel could have said, 'Well, that's great. Let's wait and see *if* God does what He has promised.' Instead it says he prayed, pleaded and fasted in sackcloth and ashes before God. In other words his faith in God was active. It would have been so easy for us in any faith walk to say, 'Let's wait and see if God will do it,' but real faith will always be seen in action. Like Daniel, faith involves listening to what God is saying. It may involve us in much prayer and perhaps even fasting. It will certainly involve us being obedient to all that God says as well as actively trusting God to fulfil His promise. In the Bible when the disciples came to Jesus with a need of five thousand hungry men, besides women and children, Jesus got the disciples actively involved in seeing the miracle happen. Matthew 14 records how Jesus asked the disciples to bring the fish and loaves to Him, then after prayer He put the food into the hands of the disciples and the disciples gave it to the people. If the disciples had not put their obedience and faith into action then a miracle would not have happened. If we want to see our faith grow then we need to be obedient and activate our faith. It is important to realise, though, that our faith must not come from our action, but rather our action must come from our faith in God.

A number of months later, it would have been easy to give up and not be active on one of our journeys of faith. We were in the middle of planning our short-term team training when we got a phone call to say that the school we had hired for the week had made a mistake and had double-booked us. As their other client had initially booked the time first, they were apologising for the mistake and asking if we could change our dates. Unfortunately we could not do that as our advertising had already gone out and so they were advising us to book elsewhere. I remember a couple of our leaders telling us about the phone call and saying, 'Well, I guess that means we have to get back to the drawing board and find somewhere else.' Ray immediately said, 'Before we do anything, we need to go back to God and see what He is saying. If He says we should find somewhere else, then fine, but if God says that this is the place for us, then somehow He will give us the school for the dates we need.'

We immediately went back to God in prayer. During that prayer meeting God impressed on us that we should fast and pray and at the same time phone the school and see if we could share the building with their other client. When we suggested this to the school, they said that they reckoned it would be impossible for us to share the building and they did not feel they wanted to suggest this to their other client – however, they would get back to us on the Monday with a definite answer. When Monday arrived and no phone call came it was a testing time for us all. We needed to actively hold on to God and trust Him for a miracle. On the Tuesday the school phoned and left a message saying that we could have the building to ourselves; we did not need to share. We never did discover what had happened, we were just thankful that as we activated our faith, God stepped in and again showed us that it is always right to first listen to Him, even when doors firmly close in your face.

During the writing of this book, a young drummer called Joe who is in our band 'Steve', and who has only been with us in ngm for the last nine months, has walked through an amazing journey of faith. Let me tell you his story.

Joe joined ngm in September 2002 with financial support of £105 per month from people within his home church. He knew that if he was going to survive month by month he needed to put his faith into action and believe God for the money he needed to pay for food and every-day expenses. When a few months later he joined the ngm band 'Steve', he and Paul O'Connor, the bass guitarist, started to pray and fast for a house they could rent together. After two months of praying, God showed them the right house. They each needed £1,400 to cover the deposit, the first month's rent in advance, and letting fees. As Joe had only £100 in the bank he knew he needed a miracle. However, as they prayed, God provided every penny he needed through gifts from friends and anony-mous givers. This was the first time in his life that he had experienced God moving in this way. It was exciting.

A number of months later though, he needed to see God move in power again. The drum kit he had brought with him into ngm was beginning to show signs of its age and was not providing the sound the band needed. He and the guys in the band began to pray that God would release to Joe a much higher quality set of drums. Joe researched what drums were available and began to pray for a specific drum kit that would be perfect for his work in ngm. He found it a little daunting to discover that his perfect drum kit would cost £5,000 brand new, but he reminded himself that God had make it perfectly clear that he should be in the band. And he knew that God would fulfil His promise of equipping those who serve Him.

After praying with his family and also with the guys in 'Steve', he got a measure of a breakthrough in prayer, when a friend in ngm, Mark Bowers, loaned him a set of drums that he was not using at present. He was so grateful to Mark but knew this was only a temporary answer to prayer. He continued to pray for his own set. As time went on, however, Joe's faith started turning to hope and at times frustration. Why was God not answering his prayers? He was finding it hard to believe that God would equip him with his own kit, even though God had done so much for him already. I'm sure you can understand some of the frustrations he was going through. Perhaps God had not called him into ngm as a drummer? Maybe he was disobeying God by just following his own dreams and desires? His prayers seemed to be hitting a brick wall as he tried without success to hear what God was saying.

Joe found it very disheartening when he discovered that in the course of his work, the drums that had been so generously lent to him were being damaged. Any gifts that came in were only helping to fix the breakages. He cried out to God to show him what to do. During one of the ngm meetings he felt God challenge him to give away his own drum kit, which had been stacked in a cupboard. Even though he could have sold the kit and got some necessary money, he knew he had to obey God and do what He had told him to do. I mentioned earlier that Joe felt it was right to approach Daniel, my son, and give him his drums. As he began to realise what an answer to prayer it was for Daniel, he was encouraged to know that he had heard correctly. He reminded himself that night that no matter how hard it was, he needed to continue to trust God for his drums.

A number of weeks later Joe knew he could not go on just 'hoping' that God would do something, instead he needed some kind of breakthrough which would silence the doubts and fears. As the people in 'Steve' and the ngm music department prayed for him, there were many words of encouragement from God to continue to trust Him. At that point he also went to see Ray to ask for advice and wisdom. Ray listened to his story and then encouraged him to remember that faith is always active. He said we would pray and stand in faith with him, but really he needed to get alone with God, read his Bible and discover the next step God wanted him to take in order to see His provision.

That night Joe spent time telling God how desperate he was for His direction and told Him that he was prepared to do anything. God then told him to take a step of faith and order the two most important things he needed. He had been trying to save his pennies for a pair of custom earplugs but he knew the things he needed most were headphones and a drum stool. He knew he had to be obedient so that night he phoned and ordered the headphones and the drum stool without having enough money in the bank to pay for them. It was a very scary thing to do but he knew that he had heard God clearly and that it would have been disobedient to do nothing. The next morning, when he arrived at ngm, he was told that money had been given specifically for him to purchase a pair of headphones, a drum stool *and* a custom pair of earplugs. As usual God had given him more than he expected. As you can imagine, his faith was increasing and he eagerly went back to God for his next step.

As he prayed he felt God urge him to pray with faith and not just hope that God would give him the drums of his dreams. He had written down a specific list of what he wanted in his drum kit, even down to the colour. A number of months before he had seen a second hand kit on the Internet for £2,000 and he realised that this was the exact kit he had specified including the colour! Before he could do anything about it, the advertisement had disappeared. A few weeks later when he looked again he saw the same kit again only this time it was cheaper. Joe had prayed at the time, but had not been able to hear anything from God. The advertisement had since disappeared and then reappeared on the day he had prayed with the band.

When he prayed on the night after receiving his first three items from God, he felt God say that the drums advertised on the Internet were the set that God wanted him to have. He phoned Ray and told him about the drums and Ray encouraged him to find out the cost. That night someone in ngm gave him £100 towards his drums. The next day, after discovering that the drums were going to cost £1,700, Ray informed Joe that three gifts had just come in for him, one for £1,000 and one for £500 and one for £100. Each of the people who gave had heard God tell them to send money to Joe specifically for his drums. Joe now had the money to realise his faith goal. God gave him the kit of his dreams but it involved Joe being active in his prayers, active even through his frustrations, active in obedience and active in trusting God to see his miracle released.

A few days before all his dreams came true, God clearly showed Joe that He was not only concerned about his drums, but He was a loving faithful Father who cared about his monthly support too. While I was teaching at an event in the University of Chichester, a lady approached me and asked if it was possible to support someone through ngm. When I replied that it was and that everyone in ngm had people who give to us on a regular and irregular basis, she asked if there was a young person who was just starting out that she could support. While she talked, I was praying inwardly and asking God whose name I should give. There were many I could have mentioned as all of us in ngm reach out every month for God to help us with our every day expenses, however the name that flashed into my mind was 'Joe'. As I explained Joe's circumstances to her, she told me she wanted to support Joe by giving £50 per month. Not only has God given him the drum kit of his dreams, He has also provided a generous lady who wants to regularly support Joe with his monthly living costs. We have such a loving faithful God. As you pray, do make sure you are active in hearing from God and taking practical steps to see your faith-goal realised. Write down what God says to you and then when you have done what He has asked you to do, tick it off your list. It will encourage your faith to see each step accomplished as you continue to walk through your journey of faith.

Exercises for your faith muscles

▶ Read Luke 15:3–24. Notice how in each parable the shepherd, the woman and the father never stop looking for their lost sheep, coin or son. They are active in their faith and continue to look despite their loss. What can you learn from this about being active in your faith and not giving up?

▶ Notice from the chapter above how precious each item was to the person involved. They had a hunger in their hearts to see their sheep/coin/son brought back to themselves. Think through/discuss what can you learn from this and how this hunger can feed any faith walk.

▶ Spend some time praying the disciples' prayer from Luke 17:5: *'The apostles said to the Lord, "Increase our faith!"'* Do remember if you are on a faith journey to ask God what your next step should be.

▶ Memorise James 2:17:

> *'In the same way, faith by itself, if it is not accompanied by action, is dead.'*

Chapter 16

Faith Not Presumption

> A man thrust an envelope into our hands and said, 'God has told me to give you this.' When we opened the envelope it contained the equivalent of £170.

A number of years ago, while I was in the States preaching at various churches, God spoke to me and gave me a vision to hold a conference for women in Bristol. To be honest, I didn't usually like ladies' days or women's conferences, so it seemed unusual for me to be thinking and dreaming about such an event. As I chatted to the Lord about the event, I had a desire in me to host it at a luxury hotel rather than the usual Christian conference centre. I wanted people to be able to be pampered physically and to be toned up spiritually at the same time. I felt it was important for the hotel to have a swimming pool, spa bath, steam room, fitness room, great food, good bedrooms and quality service.

When I got back to Thornbury, I shared my dream with the rest of the leadership team and also with Ally Budd who was my personal assistant at the time. We had a look at all the local hotels and recognised that a certain one had all the facilities we needed. After much prayer, Ally and I booked an appointment with the conference manager and prayed that we would have favour as we went to see her. I explained to her that I wanted to host an event in the hotel and that the facilities this hotel had were perfect for my conference, but the prices needed to be much lower. As you can imagine, the conference prices in hotels are incredibly expensive and it was impossible to ask people to pay those huge prices. However, as we walked out of the hotel that day we realised we had a fantastic deal. God had honoured our faith and performed yet another miracle. At that point I was able to offer a weekend staying in a four-star luxury hotel, with bed and breakfast for one night and dinner bed and breakfast the next night, with all the conference fees, books etc., for £99 per person.

Now I had the deal, I just needed the people to come. Ally and I had been able to book a conference room that accommodated fifty people. Again, we prayed and stood in faith for fifty people to attend. We did not feel it was right to advertise the first event, so instead we sent out a letter to our contacts and prayer partners inviting them to attend. Within months the event was full. We managed to get the hotel to extend the numbers to sixty, but it was impossible to cater for any more that year. The conference was full months before the event took place. We had an amazing weekend where people's lives were not just challenged but changed. The following year I held two week-ends and the year after that, I moved to the large conference room in the hotel. Eventually I was running three weekends just to try and accommodate the people who wanted to attend.

We make sure that each conference is soaked in prayer. Every Tuesday for about nine months before the event we pray and fast for God to move in a powerful way at each conference. After people book in we pray for them by name, calling on God to move in their lives. During the week before the event, each of the team will fast at least one day so that we have a continuous time of fasting and continue to pray for each person by name. The results have been incredible. Many people have been set free, healed from physical and emotional complaints and brought into a new and fresh relationship with Jesus. Over the years, I have had many letters from people whose lives have been impacted by what God has done through these conferences.

Each year I ask the Lord if He wants to me continue to run these weekends. I don't want to presume that God wants me to continue year after year. As I am sure you are aware, there is a huge difference between presumption and faith. When Joshua and the children of Israel accomplished their huge walk of faith around Jericho and the walls fell down, they were on a natural high. As they stood in faith, believing God, God was faithful and performed a miracle for them. The book of Joshua tells us,

> '*So the* LORD *was with Joshua, and his fame spread throughout the land.*'   (Joshua 6:27)

However, the very next chapter explains how Joshua sent men to look at the next town and report back what they found. When they came back with the report that it was only a small town with few men, it was decided to send only a few of the army to fight against Ai. Joshua did not go to God for his advice, instead he acted in the presumption that God would again defeat their enemies. When thirty-six of the men they sent were killed and the army was defeated, Joshua could not believe it. I can imagine all the questions that Joshua would have poured out to the Lord: 'What are you doing, Lord? Didn't You tell us that You would be with us? Didn't You tell us to go and possess the land? We should never have gone on this faith walk. It is too difficult. You didn't tell me it was going to be this difficult, Lord.' Right into the middle of Joshua's complaints, God spoke and told him that someone had sinned in the camp and that that was why they had been defeated. We must be careful to walk in faith each time and not presume that just because God did it one way before, He will do it the same way again.

When Ray and I started out living by faith in 1981 for our finances, we knew that God was saying three things that were important for us – intimacy, faith and obedience. It is so important to pursue a walk of intimacy with God, so that you can listen to what He is saying in each circumstance.

After running three weekends in 2002, I prayed and told God that I would like to do one large weekend each year rather than three. I knew the hotel we were using could not accommodate all the people who wanted to come in one big weekend and therefore I started to look elsewhere.

At the same time, I also asked God to show me if I should hold a weekend conference at all in 2003. As I said earlier, I certainly did not want to walk in presumption. As I waited for God to answer me, I went with Ally to look at all the hotels in Bristol and the surrounding area to see if there was one that could accommodate the numbers. After visiting masses of hotels there was one that stood out from all the rest. We made an appointment to see the conference manager of the Marriott hotel, which is located right in the centre of the city. Again we prayed, fasted and sought God before going in to discuss dates and finances. The good news was that we received almost as good a deal as at our last venue, but the bad news was that they were fully booked up on the dates we required. We looked at several other hotels, but none had the capabilities of holding a conference of hundreds during one weekend. We were left with a dilemma. What should we do? Should we go back to the original hotel and still do three weekends; move to another hotel and do three weekends; or find somewhere else? I needed to hear God speak clearly to me. I kept asking God over and over again and would not let Him go until I had heard His voice. Jesus encourages us in Luke 18, through the story of the persistent widow, to be persistent in our prayers and not give up. I continued to persist even although I was finding it difficult to hear anything from God on this matter.

After several weeks of seeking God, Ray woke up early one morning with a word from God for me and felt that I should pray and ask God what it meant. He felt that God had said that this year would be a fallow year for my spiritual health weekends. I had been feeling quite ill during weekends two and three that particular year and had already heard from God that this year would be more like a sabbatical year for me personally; so I went to God in prayer, asking for clarity. Could God be saying that He did not want me to hold the weekends in 2003?

During one night, in the early hours of the morning, I remembered that I had held weekends for six years running and therefore 2003 would be the seventh year (the sabbatical year). When I read my Bible the next day, I could not believe what I was reading. I always read my Bible with one of my Bible planners, which means that it takes me right through the Bible each year. That morning my reading was in Exodus. God spoke to me so clearly through Exodus 31:12–17, which is all about making sure you observe the Sabbath. I felt God could be telling me that 2003 was to be a sabbatical year of rest. I read further on and then I stopped in the middle of reading to pray. I prayed, 'Lord, if You want me not to hold my weekends next year, then I lay them down right now. Show me clearly if this is what You want me to do.' I opened my eyes and began to read on. The very next verse was Exodus 34:21:

> *'Six days you shall labour, but on the seventh day you shall rest;*
> *even during the ploughing season and harvest you must rest.'*

When I read those words I knew that it would be wrong to hold my weekends in 2003 and that God was asking me to be obedient in this. It seemed crazy to stop holding the weekends when God was doing so much in those who came. I knew there were some people who came every year who would be so disappointed, but I also knew I had to be obedient to God.

I wrote a letter, explaining what God had said, to the people on our mailing list, and booked the Marriott hotel for 2004. At the time of writing this book I now have over 250 booked into that conference, eight months before the event is due to take place. I have had to go to the hotel three times and ask if we can increase the allocation of bedrooms because we have so many people wanting to attend. This has all happened with no advertising strategy. We had planned to advertise in magazines in the autumn, but we could be sold out well before that time. With my small team, I spent 24 hours in the new hotel where

my 2004 conference will be held. We booked in on the Friday
of the same weekend in 2003. As well as having a fantastic time
checking out all the wonderful facilities, we also had such
powerful times of prayer. As we prayed in the hotel, God spoke
and told us He was going to *'open the floodgates of heaven and
pour out so much blessing'* (Malachi 3:10) that we would not be
able to contain it. I know this weekend conference is going to
be extra special because we have obeyed God and have done
what He wanted us to do.

There is a verse in the Bible, which I mentioned at the
beginning of this book and which I absolutely love because it
has within itself the ingredients to make faith grow. You will
find it in James and it says this,

> *'Do not merely listen to the word, and so deceive yourselves.
> Do what it says.'*   (James 1:22)

If we want to grow in faith then we must learn not only to be
intimate with Jesus and read His Word, but we also need to
learn to be obedient and trust Him. It is easy just to read the
Word rather than live it. It is as we listen, obey and trust, that
God will open up the way for a miracle to happen.

In Joshua 3, in the Old Testament, God shows us that
obedience comes first, before He releases His power. So many
times we ask God for the power to obey, when really He wants
us to obey and then He will add His power. The children of
Israel needed to cross the river Jordan, but there was no way
across. Added to their problems was the fact that the river was
in flood at that moment in time. God told the priests to go and
stand in the river and He would do a miracle. He didn't stop
the water flowing until the priests had done what He had
commanded them to do. As the priests stood in that river, with
their faith firmly fixed on God, *'the water from upstream stopped
flowing. It piled up in a heap, a great distance away, at a town called
Adam ... '* (Joshua 3:16). They could have stood at the side of
that river for quite some time, but no miracle would have
occurred. It was only as they were obedient and continued to

obey that somewhere, out of their sight, God began to do a miracle. Slowly but surely the water started to recede and all the Israelites were able to walk across on dry ground.

I remember a number of years ago, God showed Ray and me again how important obedience is in receiving all that God has for us. We had been invited to speak in Belgium at a camp during the summer and so we thought if we took Daniel, our son, with us we could perhaps travel on to Centre Parcs in Holland afterwards for a family holiday. We prayed that God would supply us with the finance not only to pay for the holiday but also for our food etc., whilst we were there.

We were so encouraged when God provided all the money we needed for our accommodation and so we booked an apartment in Centre Parcs. As the booking in Belgium was paying for our flights, that meant that our travel costs to Belgium were covered. As we continued to pray, the organiser who had heard that we were thinking of going to Holland for a week's holiday offered to drive us to the camp and collect us at the end of the week, before taking us back to the airport in Brussels. We were so encouraged at the way God seemed to be answering our prayers. All we needed now was money for food etc. As it was a self-catering holiday, we needed finance to at least pay for our food but obviously we wanted enough to buy ice creams, postcards and anything else we might need while we were there. However, when the time came for us to leave for Belgium we only had a small amount of money, not nearly enough to cover all our expenses whilst on holiday. We prayed and God gave us an assurance in our hearts that as we went and fulfilled the mission, somehow He would answer our prayers.

We had a brilliant time in Belgium and saw God move in many ways in the people we met. God was doing so much that, to be honest, we forgot about the money we needed, but God had not forgotten. At the end of the last meeting, a man came up to Ray and me and put an envelope into our hands, telling us that he believed God had said we should have this. Inside the envelope was the equivalent of over £170. We were astounded again at God's timing and evidence of His love.

There was no one who knew of our needs. We had not mentioned the fact that we needed money at all, yet God had spoken and instructed someone to give cash to us. We had a fantastic time in Holland and came home not only with memories of a brilliant holiday, but also with a story of having proved again how faithful our God is.

Years later while we were speaking in America, God answered our prayers in a similar manner. Ray and I had been invited to speak at a 'Worship Together' conference in Nashville. At the same time, our friends Ian and Dorry Townend, who now live in the States, asked us to meet them in Florida for a holiday. As the conference was covering our flights, we prayed and asked God for a holiday in Florida with our friends. Our flights were booked and our accommodation became available when we were able to transfer to Ray's parents' time-share apartment to Florida. That meant we had covered the cost of flights and accommodation so therefore all we needed was enough money for food and of course a couple of trips to Disney World with the boys.

Ian and Dorry had said they might get their tickets before they left Boise in Idaho, but we felt that for us it was not right to do that. We knew it cost a huge amount of money to visit many of the attractions so we prayed about what we should do. We knew that Ian and Dorry would understand if we could only go to a few of the theme parks, but we did not want to be party poopers and spoil their holiday either. It would have been easy just to presume God wanted us to visit the theme parks and therefore place the cost on our credit cards, but we did not have peace about doing that. We prayed before we left our British shores that God would provide for us and give us wisdom to know what to do.

During one of Ray's seminars at Nashville he happened to mention that he and I were on our way to Florida for a holiday. After the seminar was over, a lady approached him and asked if he was planning on going to any of the Disney attractions while in Florida and if we had bought our tickets as yet. When Ray replied saying we were planning to go to Disney but had not yet bought our tickets, she gave him her name and address and told us to phone her when we reached Florida. She explained that her husband worked for Disney and was allowed to give free passes to up to five of his friends. When we arrived in Florida we were able to get into as many of the Disney attractions as we wanted for absolutely nothing. God did not provide us with money this time, but provided us with tickets, which would have cost us hundreds of pounds had we bought them. If we had acted with presumption and bought the tickets before we left England, we would have missed out on the blessing God had for us. What an answer to prayer and also what kind and generous hearts that couple displayed. God is indeed faithful.

Sometimes people who don't know God have suggested to us that these things could be coincidences. All I can tell them is that these 'coincidences' seem to happen to us again and again and again. If they had only happened to us a few times, then perhaps you could put it down to coincidence. But for these things to have happened thousands of times, not only to us but also to the many people working with ngm and to thousands of other people across the world, can no longer be put down to coincidence. We have to put it down to a God who is not only real, but who also cares about the smallest of details in our lives.

Exercises for your faith muscles

Read Joshua 3 and answer the following questions:

▶ When the nation of Israel reached the river Jordan they could have presumed that God would do the same as He did with the Red Sea, but they did not. It was so important for Joshua and the nation of Israel to hear the word of God for them at that moment in time. What can we learn from this?

▶ Notice that God told the priests to stand in the river (Joshua 3:8). Standing at the side of the river would not have been enough. What can we learn from this?

▶ Notice that it says in Joshua 3:15 that the river was in flood. In other words the worst time of all to be in faith that God would stop the water. What can we learn from this about continuing to believe God rather than the circumstances around us?

▶ Notice that it says in Joshua 3:16 that the water from upstream stopped flowing and piled up in a heap at a town called Adam – a great distance away. We realise from this that as the priests stood in the river – somewhere out of their sight God was doing a miracle. It was not yet seen by them. We do not know how long they had to stand in their faith and believe God – but we do know that as they trusted, God did a miracle and eventually they saw that miracle happen. What does this teach us about standing firm in our faith?

▶ Memorise Habakkuk 2:4:

   '... the righteous will live by his faith.'

Chapter 17

Faith for Promises

> 'Hosea 1:6 – what on earth does that say?'

Ray and I had been praying for some time as to whether it was right for us to have another child. We already had a fantastic son called Daniel who was a toddler at the time. He had brought so much joy into our lives and we wanted to know from God if it was right to try for another baby. We were leading a growing ministry and I was still in the band Heartbeat at the time, so we wanted to be sure that having another baby was the correct thing to do. However, as we prayed, God did not seem to answer. It did not matter how much we stormed the heavens, it seemed as though the heavens were closed and no answer was forthcoming. Until one day – 1st April – I remember it well. We were visiting some friends in London and went with them to their church. During the service, Daniel started to get restless so I took him outside to play. While I was watching him, I prayed again to the Lord, 'God, please, would You speak to me. I really want to know if I am going to have another baby.' Even before I had finished saying the words, God's answer flashed into my mind. I heard Him say, 'Hosea chapter 1 verse 6.' I thought to myself what on earth does that say? I couldn't even remember what the book of Hosea was about, never mind knowing what verse 6 said.

So with curiosity in my heart, I picked up Daniel and walked

back into the church. I gave Daniel to Ray and opened my Bible
at Hosea 1:6 and read these words,

'Gomer conceived again and gave birth to a daughter.'

I could not believe what I was reading. God again spoke to me
and whispered, 'I am not promising you a daughter but I am
promising you that you will conceive again and you will give
birth to a child.' I turned to Ray and told him what had just
happened and what God had said. As he read the scripture he
too was convinced that God was indeed speaking.

With renewed passion in our hearts, we knew it was right to
try for another child. God had spoken and therefore it would
happen. However, as the months and years passed by without
me conceiving it was hard to hold on to that word. God had
said I would conceive again and yet no matter how hard we
tried, I could not manage to become pregnant. We could not
understand it. Why was God's word not coming into being?
Had we heard correctly? Was there something wrong? The
doctors confirmed that there was nothing physically wrong
and no medical reason as to why I was not conceiving, but as
the years passed by the 'word from God' was becoming more
difficult to believe.

Eventually at the age of 40, I took my precious word from
God to our good friend Ken McGreavy. On one of our visits to
see Ken and his wife Hazel, I shared with them the word I had
received from God. I told Ken that I didn't understand why
God was not bringing into being that which He had promised.
I asked Ken several questions: 'Did I hear wrong? Was it the
enemy speaking to me? Did I interpret the verse in the wrong
way?' I even asked jokingly, 'Was God playing an "April fool"
on me – as it was 1st April when I heard God speak?' Ken
dismissed each one of my suggestions with a reason as to
why it was wrong. I said in desperation 'Then what is the
answer?' Ken's reply seemed to echo throughout the room
where we were meeting. 'Well, all I can say is – perhaps it is still
to happen.'

After the initial silence I laughed and said, 'But Ken, I'm forty!' I felt a little like Sarah in the Bible who after hearing that God was going to give her a child in her old age, laughed and said, *'will I now have this pleasure?'* (Genesis 18:12). I didn't even know if I wanted another child in my forties. What if the child was deformed? Was it safe to conceive after forty? Loads of questions filled my mind but after praying with Ray we decided that if it happened it happened, but if it didn't, then there would be some questions we would have for the Lord when we got to heaven. It had been the clearest word I had ever had and we could not understand why it was not coming into being.

Three years later, however, whilst still hanging on to Hosea 1:6, at the age of forty-three, God's promise came into being. I conceived again and on my birthday gave birth to a fantastic little boy called Aidan Jon Goudie. He was the best birthday present I have ever had.

During those seven or so years where we had the promise but not the fulfilment it was hard to cling on to God and believe Him for something that was out of my control to bring into being. There was nothing we could do other than the obvious to make it happen. Time after time my doctor would advise me to take precautions as I was now over forty and therefore, in her opinion, should not get pregnant. When I said I did not want to use any form of contraception and would be open to having another child, she would expound the reasons why there was a high probability that if I did become pregnant then the child would be disabled in some way. Try as she might she could not convince me to take precautions. I knew that if I did so then I would be disobeying God. If God's word was true and if I had heard correctly then I did not actively want to go against what God had promised. I wanted to give God every opportunity to bring His word into being. Even after I conceived I was told again and again that there was a high risk of the baby being a Down's Syndrome child because of my age. I was asked at least three times if I wanted an abortion or if I wanted a test just to check that the baby was all right. I declined all offers, as I knew that even if the baby were a Down's Syndrome child, I would not abort it. Again and again 'words' were spoken that challenged God's word to me but as we held out in faith and believed God, He gave Ray and me a wonderful, healthy, gorgeous little baby boy.

It's so easy to let the word of God 'go' in your situation when problems and difficulties arise, especially when you don't understand why God's word to you is not coming into being. You do everything you should – you pray, fast, and seek God but nothing seems to happen. Questions like 'Where is God? Why isn't He working? Why aren't His promises coming into being?' arise again and again. The question that the enemy flung at me at the beginning of my journey of faith for Aidan was 'Did God say you would have another child?' In the garden of Eden, many years ago, the enemy confronted Eve with the same question, 'Did God say?' The enemy will always question God's words by trying to put doubts and fears in your way. When we are filled with doubts and fears it is not easy to fly high in faith, in fact those doubts and fears seem to make us crash land with a huge bump. It's at this point that we need to cling on to God's word and get beside someone who can help us to reject the garbage and begin to feel our spirits being fuelled again with faith.

I have since prayed for several people who have been trying to have a family and yet for various reasons they have not been able to conceive. I met such a couple in Houston, Texas when I was speaking at a conference. They approached me for prayer and told me their story. They were desperate to have a child and yet despite the fact that they had tried for two years, they could not conceive. Tears of frustration and confusion were often in their eyes as friends and family were able to conceive yet they had not been able to do so. It is so hard to see others conceive and have babies when you are trying everything you can to have one yourself. As they told me their story my heart went out to them. I knew exactly how they felt. They had seen a doctor, who had recommended them to try a fertility drug, but they had felt peace in their hearts in waiting until July and if nothing happened before then, then they would consider this course of action.

When they heard me preach in Houston on the subject of faith, their own faith in God was increased. As they chatted together at the end of the meeting they opened up to each other in a way they hadn't for a long time. They were completely honest about how they felt and after they had prayed and cried together, they felt from God that they should approach me to pray for them. As I prayed I knew that the same God who had given my son, Aidan, life could do the same for them. After we prayed I encouraged them to look to our amazing faithful God. When I next heard from Leena and Binoy, it was to tell me that God had answered their prayers. Leena discovered in the July that she was pregnant. She gave birth in March 2002 to a beautiful little girl, Alyssa Anne, almost a year to the day that we had prayed in Houston. Both Leena and Binoy were ecstatic about their little girl but felt that God had also promised them a boy. I encouraged them to continue to put their faith in God and if God had indeed spoken then He would not fail to fulfil His promise. She wrote to me recently to tell me that once again God had been faithful to His promise. She is pregnant and has just found out that she is expecting a boy.

Another couple that struggled to conceive was Alison and Simon McKinna. Alison heard me speak at one of my spiritual health weekends. During that weekend I shared the story of Aidan and how God had been faithful to a promise He had given me years earlier. Afterwards Alison approached me and asked me if I would pray for her and her husband. She explained that they had been trying to conceive unsuccessfully for two years. As we chatted I could see the longing in her eyes to have a baby of her own, but she told me that the doctors had just diagnosed her as having polycystic ovarian syndrome. As this condition makes conception extremely difficult she had asked a few close friends to pray that God would somehow intervene and bless them with a child. I prayed with her and asked God to bless her with a child of her own. I encouraged her to put God at the centre of her life, to delight in God and who He is. I felt that as she did so, God would give her the desire of her heart (Psalm 37:4).

She wrote to tell me that she and her husband had found that word very challenging. As she read the Bible and prayed, she really struggled with deep conflicting emotions, but as she kept putting God at the centre of her life and of her desires, she felt God's amazing power sustaining her and strengthening her. A short three months later she conceived, and their gorgeous little son, Robert, was born prematurely at the end of that same year. He is a fantastic little boy and is a huge blessing to them both. They certainly did receive the desire of their hearts. A few months ago I saw them at a spiritual health day I was holding at our complex in Thornbury. When she told me they were trying again to conceive, my prayer that day was 'God give them a double portion of your blessing.' She wrote to tell me a few weeks ago that she has conceived again and is expecting another child soon. God is indeed faithful.

If you are holding on to a promise from God, don't allow circumstances or the lies of the enemy to release your grip on God. Keep close to Him and keep listening to all He is saying. Remember, it says in Ephesians that after we have done everything we should *'stand firm'* (Ephesians 6:13). It is good to note, however, as faith is always active, that even our standing on God's word should be an active thing. We should stand trusting, clinging, praising and believing our loving and faithful God.

Exercises for your faith muscles

▶ Read Proverbs 3:5–6. It is easy in any faith walk to put our focus on the goal and on what we are aiming for rather than keeping our focus on God. What can we learn from these two verses about this?

▶ Meditate on Psalm 145:13b. Write down/discuss what you receive through this meditation.

▶ Has God promised you something you have yet to receive? If so, spend some time asking God to reveal more of His heart about this and write down what He says. (Do make sure that God has indeed spoken and promised and that it is not just your own thoughts or desires.)

▶ Memorise Psalm 145:13b:

> *'The LORD is faithful to all his promises*
> *and loving towards all he has made.'*

Chapter 18

Adventure of Faith

'I am going to give you a missions and arts complex. Do not worry about the money, instead birth it in prayer.'

For years we had housed our offices and our studio in other peoples' buildings. I mentioned earlier that in Malmesbury, where we had been based for ten years, the Shaftsbury Society had been extremely kind to us and given us the use of a flat, and latterly an old barn, which we changed into our studio for a peppercorn rent. When we moved to Bristol in 1993, the Bristol Christian Fellowship very kindly gave us the use of a building in the centre of Bristol where we could put our studios. They also allowed us to rent some rooms from them in their beautiful manor house, which then became our offices. After being there for some time, we felt it was right to begin to pray and ask God for premises of our own. After some weeks of praying Ray and I felt God say to us that He was going to give us a missions and arts complex. We knew we were in for a big walk of faith; little did we realise what a *huge* walk of faith we were embarking upon. We thought we were praying for God to supply around £200,000 in order for us to buy a house in which we could have our offices and perhaps change the garage into a studio. We were thinking small. God, however, was thinking *big*. Our journey of faith led us to believe God not for £200,000 but for £3 million pounds.

If we had known at the beginning that our missions and arts complex would cost £3 million I am sure that our faith walk would not have started. God knew that it was best to let us know the information bit by bit, and as we trusted Him for one bit of the plan, He then led us to the next part. One thing I have discovered throughout all our walks of faith is that God is wise and He knows our frailties. Right at the commencement of our 'journey' God told us 'not to worry about the money but to birth the project in prayer.' It was good that He said that, because at that precise moment in time we did not have one penny towards our faith goal. I was pregnant at the time and my pregnancy became a prophetic symbol as to what God was saying. The fact that I was pregnant was a miracle and we knew that as we birthed this project in prayer, the outcome of this would be a miracle too.

We had early-morning prayer meetings, late-night prayer meetings and prayer meetings during the day, all asking God to show us where we could find our missions and arts complex. As we continued to pray, God continued to stretch our faith. As well as praying and fasting, we began to look to see what property was available in the local area. Without having any money in our bank account we visited several homes that were up for sale to see if we could find where God wanted us to have our missions and arts centre, but they were either too small or too far out of town. Through our activity and our prayer sessions God began to show us that He wanted to give us property within Thornbury itself.

One night Ray and I received a phone call from two of our close friends who told us that they had heard from God. They wanted to give us a donation towards our 'Caedmon' project (this project was named Caedmon after a Celtic bard by that name who was known for writing songs that reached into the culture of that day). We were excited and very encouraged. We weren't sure how much they would give, we thought perhaps a few thousand pounds, but when we heard that the 'donation' was £1 million we were overwhelmed. Praise God for people like John and Rose Lancaster who not only saw our dedicated prayers and understood our hearts but took time to hear from God, saw the vision, believed in it and were prepared to partner with us.

When we heard that we had been given £1 million I turned to Ray and said, 'A million pounds! We could buy the whole of Thornbury for that!' I thought we would have no problem finding the correct place but I was woefully wrong. In fact it took us years to find the right site.

You should have seen the ngm team when we released the news to them. To begin with there was shocked silence and then a roar of joy as the news sunk in. A million pounds! We'd have no problem now – little did we know that we were only at the beginning of an amazing walk of faith which would end with a building that would be a testimony to God's amazing love and faithfulness.

Ray contacted many local farmers, asking them if they had thought about selling their properties. It seemed crazy to be phoning people up who we didn't know to ask if they wanted to sell their farms. The reactions from people Ray spoke to were varied. Some were bemused, others angry and annoyed thinking we were acting on behalf of estate agents; but most were just not interested. We did visit various farm buildings that were on the market to see if we could house our complex there, only to find that they were not suitable. We looked at numerous buildings in the centre of Thornbury but none of them were big enough for what God wanted to do. After some time I remember the estate agents telling us that the place we were looking for in Thornbury just did not exist. When we visited the planning department they told us that even if we did find a place to buy, they would not give us planning permission for what we wanted to do. Even some church leaders told us to go to the north of England to build our missions and arts complex because there was plenty of land there. At times like those we felt discouraged and went back to God in prayer: 'Are You really telling us You will give us a missions and arts complex, Lord? Have we got this all wrong? Do You want us to look north? Are the church leaders right –

should we move our headquarters to the north of England?' Each time we went back to God in prayer, God confirmed again and again that He was going to give us a missions and arts complex right here in Thornbury near the centre of the town.

At one point a good friend of ours, Wayne Drain, came to visit. Before he left he gave us an encouraging prophetic word about our complex. He had felt God say to him that the complex would be near the centre of town, surrounded by trees and set on a hill. We held all these 'words' and scriptures that were given to us in our hearts and kept continuing to encourage each other to trust God despite the circumstances. Throughout these years we visited many properties but we could not find the one that God had for us. I remember Ray getting into his car several times and praying, 'Lord direct me like You did those Celtic saints of old when the wind blew their boats to the shores where You wanted them to go. Blow by the wind of Your Spirit and direct this car to the property You want to give us.' You can just imagine Ray sitting in the car saying, 'Okay, Lord, which way do I go, right or left?' Even through our foolishness we were genuinely saying to God, 'We want to hear Your voice and be directed by You.' However, Ray could not find the property that was for us. We got the distinct impression when we prayed that God was saying that we could not see the property at present but that it did exist and that God would show us soon.

As I previously said, we felt that my pregnancy was like a prophetic sign as to what God was going to do. When Aidan Jon Goudie was born on my birthday, Ray thought perhaps God would show us where the property was on that day but again we were disappointed when that didn't happen. Eventually, in 1997, we received a prophetic word from one of our prayer partners at our ngm open day that said, 'the gates will open in 1998', and that was exactly what happened. Through a remarkable set of circumstances, on my and Aidan's birthday, 27th February 1998, we found the right house. It was a beautiful old manor house which had fantastic gardens. It is set on a small hill, surrounded by trees, near the centre of town, right next door to a Tesco supermarket. When we stood in the building with our friends, John and Rose Lancaster, all four of us just knew that this was the correct place.

We had been unaware that this superb property even existed. A high wall, with large wrought iron gates that were boarded up by wood so no one could see through, surrounded the property. The owner and his wife who had lived in this massive building did not want to encourage any visitors and so made sure that the gates were always shut. No wonder Ray and I could not find it and yet we had passed its walls every day.

Our first contact with the owner was when we wrote a letter to him asking if he was interested in selling his property to us. He did not have the property up for sale, however he said that if we would meet his price then he would sell the house to us. We discovered on our first visit to see him that a firm of solicitors had also asked him if he was willing to sell and he had given them ten days in which to come back to him to let him know if they would meet his price. When we confirmed with him a week later that we would go ahead, he told us that the firm of solicitors had come back and said they wanted the house. He had told them that he had another party interested now and as they had not come back to him within the ten days he would not sell to them without giving us the first option. Despite the fact that they wanted to increase their offer, the owner stood by his word and by the grace of God we were able to purchase the building.

When we eventually got the keys to the house on 22nd June 1998, the first thing we did was to 'open the gates' and remove the wood from behind the gates so that people could see into the driveway.

When God speaks and gives a promise, He will always fulfil it despite the problems that may surround it. God will always find a way of honouring His promises. Some of you reading this book right now might be at a place where you are waiting for God to fulfil His promises. Can I encourage you to keep going and not give up because God will indeed be faithful to you? Do make sure again and again that God has indeed spoken and keep going back to Him in prayer to find out what His instructions are. As I have said before, in any faith walk there are three ingredients that are vital: intimacy, obedience and trust. We must take time to listen to God's instructions, obey what He has said, and keep our eyes firmly fixed on Him so that our faith will not waver. In Joshua 3:3–4 God told the Israelites to keep their eyes on Him and on what He was doing because they had *'never been this way before'*. During our walk of faith, God constantly reminded us to do the same. We can so easily take our eyes off the Lord and put them onto our circumstances. When we do that, as Peter found out in Matthew 14:30, our faith flies out of the window and we begin to sink.

Exercises for your faith muscles

Read Matthew 14:22–32.

► This story shows again how three ingredients are essential to developing our faith: *hearing* from God, *obedience* to God and *trusting* in God. Peter heard Jesus say *'Come,'* (Matthew 14:29). He immediately put his faith into action and obeyed what Jesus said. He then trusted in Jesus and began to walk. None of the other disciples stepped out of the boat – only Peter. What does this teach us about faith?

► The moment Peter took his eyes off Jesus his faith disappeared. Matthew 13:30 tells us that when he looked at the circumstances around him he began to sink. Doubts and fears can so often find a resting place in us if we do not keep our eyes on Jesus. Think through and write down/ discuss what this means in our journey of faith with God.

► Even when Peter did doubt, he immediately knew that in order to resume his walk of faith he needed help from Jesus. We all go through doubts and fears from time to time. What does this chapter teach us to do?

▶ Memorise Hebrews 12:2:

> *'Let us fix our eyes on Jesus, the author and perfecter of our faith, who for the joy set before him endured the cross, scorning its shame, and sat down at the right hand of the throne of God.'*

Chapter 19

Eyes of Faith

'I'm sorry Nancy – but the deal is off! The seller has pulled out!'

I couldn't quite believe what I was hearing. A number of weeks after our offer had verbally been agreed I received a phone call from our estate agent who told me, 'I am really sorry, Nancy, to bring you such bad news, but the deal is off. The seller has pulled out.' I was stunned. Ray was in Germany at the time speaking to a number of church leaders on the subject of faith. When I called him to tell him the bad news, he had just finished telling the leaders what God had done with us and encouraging them to keep going in their faith and to trust God no matter what. Neither he nor I could believe that the sellers had pulled out especially when our estate agent had told us that there seemed to be no reason for doing so. The sellers had just decided that they no longer wished to sell. Ray and I agreed that we would pray and see what God was saying.

I called each of our ngm leadership team and asked them to come and pray and fast with me. The four of us gathered together in our home to pray and afterwards I went for a walk on my own to pray. I could not understand what God was doing. 'Did You not say, God, that You would provide a missions and arts centre? Is this not the right place? God, what are You playing at?' All the time I was praying I kept hearing the words in my mind, *'Why are you crying out to me? Tell the sons of Israel to move on.'* I said 'Yes, Yes, Lord, but what are You doing?' Eventually, I opened my Bible and looked to see where those words came from. I found them in Exodus 14:15.

Moses had been trusting God as he led the children of Israel out of Egypt. Things went well for a while and then suddenly, after being careful to follow God's instructions, Moses found himself and the whole nation of Israel at the edge of the Red Sea. As he contemplated what God could be asking him to do, he suddenly heard in the distance the rumble of the Egyptian troops coming to murder and destroy them. There was no way forward and there was no way back. Right at that point, the children of Israel complained, grumbled and accused Moses of bad leadership. Moses cried out to God and the Lord replied saying,

> *'Why are you crying out to me? Tell the Israelites to move on.'*
> (Exodus 14:15)

As I read that story I asked God, 'Are You telling me that You are going to open up the sale again? If You are Lord, would You give that verse to Ray in Germany?' I phoned Ray and told him I had had a verse of Scripture from the Lord. He almost stopped me there and then because God had given him the same passage of Scripture in Germany. We felt we should do what Moses did and 'Stand and see the salvation of our God' (see Exodus 13:14).

Ray arrived home on Sunday evening and on the Monday morning I received a phone call from our estate agent, saying, 'Nancy, you are not going to believe this, but it is all back on again.' Before I could stop myself I said, 'David, I am not surprised!' When he asked me what I meant I explained to this man, who was not a Christian and yet had seen God move in many ways throughout this whole project, that God had spoken to us during Friday and Saturday and had told us that the deal would be on again.

When you go on a faith walk, you will discover that at times

you will have to cling on to God's words despite the circumstances. In the natural it looked as if the deal was closed and we
had lost the house, but looking at it through the eyes of God
this was not the case. It is not unusual to encounter problems
and difficulties when you go on a faith walk. The question is
how are you going to deal with them? Are you going to believe
God, as Moses did, stretch your hand over the waters and allow
God to make a way through the sea? It's very scary and I am
sure you will appreciate what Moses must have gone through.
If God had not acted, Moses would have been dead and his
journey of faith finished. Victory lay in his obedience to God's
words. It says:

> '*Moses stretched out his hand over the sea, and all that night the*
> LORD *drove the sea back ... and turned it into dry land.*'
> (Exodus 14:21)

It is worth noting that when Moses raised his hand, the miracle
didn't happen immediately, the Bible quite clearly says that '*all
that night the* LORD *drove the sea back*'! We live in such an instant
world where we expect things to happen immediately. It is not
always so in the Kingdom of God. Moses had to keep his eyes
firmly on God and keep his faith and trust intact during that
long, hard night. But as he did, God did a miracle. Can you
imagine how he must have felt? The Egyptians had not gone
away, the danger was constantly there, the people were still
grumbling and complaining; however, God had spoken. Moses
put his trust in God despite the horrendous circumstances.
Even if at first we don't see anything happening, do remember
that it's as we keep listening, obeying and trusting in God that
God will do His part and we will see our 'Red Sea' open up!
Our God is indeed faithful!

After a number of weeks, when we had purchased the house
with the £1 million we were given, we thought our journey of
faith was over. However, God then spoke and said, 'Now I want
you to build your missions and arts centre on the grounds of
this house.' It's important to realise that sometimes when we

think our faith journey should end, that's in fact when it is only just beginning. God was telling us that there was more ground to occupy.

Exercises for your faith muscles

► Have you ever been on a faith journey where you have had to trust God despite the circumstances? If so, think through/discuss the situation and how you overcame all the obstacles. If not, spend some time asking God to increase your faith and help you keep your eyes on Him.

► Think through/discuss how easy it is to give up when problems and difficulties cross our path on our journey of faith through life. Meditate on 2 Chronicles 15:7: *'But as for you, be strong and do not give up, for your work will be rewarded.'* Write down/discuss what you receive from God through this meditation.

► Paraphrase 2 Corinthians 4:18. Put this verse into your own words.

► Memorise 2 Corinthians 5:7:

  'We live by faith and not by sight.'

Chapter 20

Faith to the End

> 'Are You telling me, Lord, that You are not going to turn up on Friday and that our Caedmon project is dead?'

There was much joy when we moved into our new premises. We decided to hold a celebration each year on the day we received the keys to thank God for all He had done for us. We felt it should be a celebration where we would tell the many stories of God's faithfulness to us so that each new person in ngm would hear the facts of God's amazing grace to us. Every 22nd June, we have a fun-filled day for everyone in ngm. All of us, including our children, come and have great fun on the bouncy castles and the inflatable obstacle races we bring into our grounds. We supply food, drink and ice-cream for everyone and then we worship, tell the stories, and thank God for all He has done for us. It is a good way of reminding ourselves of the amazing adventure of faith we have been on and what a wonderful, faithful God we serve.

In the Bible God encouraged the children of Israel to tell their descendants of the amazing miracles that He had done for them. The reason for this is that God knows we so easily forget. At many points throughout the Bible we see the Israelites forgetting God's faithfulness to them again and again. We often imagine that we would never be like that, but it is so easy to do the same. We all need to be reminded of God's love and faithfulness to us even when we have at times been faithless to Him.

As we celebrated God's amazing goodness to us, we were also thinking of the road ahead that God was still asking us to walk on. What were we going to find there? How were we going to find the money that we needed for the next portion of our journey? And yet even before we had time to remind ourselves that God had said at the beginning of the journey, 'Do not worry about the finance, just birth it in prayer', we were given a donation for the next phase of the building project – of £500,000.

At that point we thought that £500,000 would complete the building that we were going to call Caedmon. However, when we went to our architects and builders we discovered that it would take another £1,500,000 (approximately) to complete our missions and arts complex. We continued to pray and small amounts of money from our supporters came in. Our trustees, Ken and Hazel McGreavy and Richard Collier-Keywood were incredibly supportive and we so valued the prayer, advice and wisdom that they gave. Together with them we agreed to start building our complex even though we did not have the money to complete it. We had felt God say that we should put our faith into action and build as much as we could for the money we had. We split our project into two halves. It was estimated that phase 1 would cost us just over £500,000 and we knew that if we did not have enough for the rest of the building then we could stop there and wait until we had the finance to progress with phase 2. It was so good to know that in our trustee board we had people of integrity who were with us on the journey; their support meant so much to Ray and me.

When we visited the local planning department and submitted our plans we were told categorically that we would not get planning permission to build this building. The chief planner himself decided to oppose it. As always, with any opposition we encountered, we went back to God in prayer. We took our example from Nehemiah who encountered so many problems in the building work that God had called him to do, but each time he encountered a problem he first and foremost went to God in prayer. As he did so, God overcame each problem.

Eventually our planning application came up to the planning committee. The chief planner was there to tell the councillors why this building should not be built. Ray was given two minutes to explain why he thought it should go ahead. We knew that without God, the planning permission, which we needed, would not be given. All of us in ngm prayed and fasted and sought God for a miracle. In faith we bought the champagne to celebrate and prayed like crazy that we would not need to keep it in the box. However, Ray came back to tell us that despite the opposition, God had won the day and the permission had been granted. Again and again, God has shown us that even when the situation seems impossible, He can change the circumstances and bring about a miracle.

No matter what you are going through, put your trust in our mighty God. He is able to do abundantly above all that you can ask or even think of (Ephesians 3:20). What seems impossible to us is no problem to Him. How we needed to keep that in mind when the £500,000 was nearly gone.

We had almost completed phase 1 of our building but we still needed approximately £120,000. And then when we had paid that, we needed another £1,000,000 or so to complete phase 2. Over a period of months we had been praying for God to supply us with what we needed. Bit by bit small donations came in, but we still needed approximately £100,000. The builders had given us a deadline but as each deadline approached they would change the date and we would realise that we had another few weeks to see God answer our prayers. However, eventually the builders told us that a certain date was the last deadline and that they really needed the money by that time.

As we continued to pray there were times when our faith was low and we would despair as to where we could possibly find the money that we needed. I remember one time when the devil came and whispered in my ear, 'You are going to have egg all over your face when God does not supply the finance you need.' I even felt him remind me of a passage in Luke:

> *'Suppose one of you wants to build a tower. Will he not first sit down and estimate the cost to see if he has enough money to complete it? For if he lays the foundation and is not able to finish it, everyone who sees it will ridicule him, saying, "This fellow began to build and was not able to finish."'*
>
> (Luke 14:28–30)

We had a huge sign put up by our builders outside our building, advertising that there was going to be a 'mission and arts pop school' (as they called it) built on the premises. The enemy took great delight in telling me that 'Everyone in the area will hear what a disaster this will be.' Time and time again we had to tell the enemy to get lost and declare that our faith and trust was in our God.

As the deadline crept closer, we got a phone call from two special friends of ours who used to be with us in Heartbeat but who now live in the States. Ian and Dorry Townend phoned to say that a millionaire-friend of theirs would like us to come and visit him to chat about the work of ngm. Dorry told us that it seemed as though he and his wife were really keen on the Caedmon project and were prepared to fly us over so that we could chat with them. She told us 'You never know, this might be the answer to your prayers.' As Ray was already going to the States to speak at an event called 'Worship Together', I decided to meet him over there and together we would go and visit Ian and Dorry's friends.

On the evening that they invited us for a meal we brought all our leaflets and information on ngm. Although we had a fantastic night with some great people who were very interested in ngm and what our ministry was about, they did not seem interested in the Caedmon project at all. We left that evening wondering why God had brought us all the way to Boise, Idaho.

The next day, Ian and Dorry received a phone call from another couple that they had just met a few weeks previously.

When they heard that we were visiting from England, they asked if we would go for a barbecue at their home. As we travelled to their home that evening we were amazed to discover that this couple were millionaires as well. We immediately thought that perhaps this was why God had brought us to Idaho. However, even though we had an amazing barbecue and we had a brilliant time getting to know these people, not one of our prayers was realised. Although this couple were very interested in what we were doing and asked many questions about the Caedmon project and how much money we needed and by when, we left that night without having received a penny.

The next morning, we were flying to San Francisco to meet a church leader there. When we arrived at the airport he told us that he had arranged for us to have a meal that night with a couple of his friends who were billionaires. It seems like a fairy story, but within three days we had met two millionaires and one billionaire! Surely we would receive an answer to our prayers this time. When Ray and I were praying before we went out for the meal, we both felt God tell us that He did not want us to talk about the Caedmon project to these people unless they asked us about it. Well, you can guess what I was praying about during that meal! 'Lord, please get them to ask us about the Caedmon project!' During the meal they asked us all about our work; all about our missions, our teams, our bands and artists and about what Ray and I were doing, but not once throughout that evening did he or his wife ask us about the Caedmon project.

When we left that evening, tears started flowing down my face. 'Lord, what are You doing?' I cried. Ray and I were both confused and to be honest, disappointed. We could not understand why God had not provided. We could not believe that God had allowed us to meet two millionaires and one billionaire and yet we hadn't received one penny of the money we desperately needed. It was only when the whole project was over that we came to recognise that receiving no money from these three sources was in God's plan for us at that time. God

was teaching us to keep our eyes on Him despite the disap-
pointments. The next morning as I picked up my Bible, I
turned to my daily reading. As I mentioned before, since 1979
I have always used a Bible reading-planner to read the Bible.
That day, as I turned to the chapter I should read, I realised that
it was a chapter on which I had spoken many times. In fact I
had recorded a video called *Dealing with Disappointment* where I
taught on that very chapter – John 11 – using the story of Mary,
Martha and Lazarus.

I said to the Lord, 'Are You telling me, Lord, that just as You
did not turn up for the funeral of Lazarus, You are not going to
turn up for us on Friday? Are You telling me that on Friday we
are going to have to bury the Caedmon project?' Clearly I
heard God reply and say, 'Nancy, I will tell you what I told
Martha, 'If you believe you will see the glory of God' (John
11:40). As Ray and I chatted together and discussed this
chapter of the Bible, we knew we were going home with no
money. However, we realised that what we had was better than
money.

When we arrived back in Britain, the first thing we did was to
call the ngm leadership team to our home. They were all
expecting us to tell them how God had answered our prayers
and provided at least £100,000. We explained to them that we
did not have the money, but what we did have was 'a word
from God'. From there Ray went to a meeting with our project
manager and the builders where he told them we did not have
the money to continue, and therefore they would have to stop
working on the building. They listened to what Ray was saying
and then explained that they had some work on site that
would keep them there until the end of the month. They said
they would begin to close the project down, but if we received
the money before the end of the month then they would carry
on building and not close the whole project down. Obviously if
the builders then closed down the project, it would ultimately
cost us even more to start it up again.

We called a team meeting where we told everyone in ngm
what had happened. As Ray and I drove to that meeting we had

heavy hearts and wondered how the team would react. Our fears were that they would get so discouraged and disappointed when they discovered that God had not provided the money we needed. Our fears, however, were never realised. When we told them the story of what had happened to us in the States and then asked them to join us in prayer, I was amazed and so encouraged by their prayers. I have to say I have never been in such a faith-filled prayer meeting. Afterwards, as Ray and I drove back home, I turned to him and said, 'You know, Ray, I've got the £100,000 – and not only that but I have the £1 million as well.' Ray's response was 'I have too.' For the first time, both of us received the money in our spirits. We did not know how God was going to bring the finance to us, but we were convinced that somehow He was going to do it. At last we were experiencing real faith. In Hebrews 11 real faith is described like this:

> *'Now faith is being sure of what we hope for and certain of what we do not see.'*   (Hebrews 11:1)

As I have said before there is a huge difference between *hoping* that God will do something and having the faith to know for *certain* that God will do it. So many of us 'hope' and then get disappointed when it doesn't happen, but faith is knowing that God has said it and therefore He will do it. We weren't just hoping that somehow we would get the money, we just knew deep within our spirits, with complete assurance in our hearts, that we had the finance needed to finish the project.

A few days later, Ray and I got a phone call from our friends, John and Rose Lancaster, who asked if they could come and see us. God had spoken to them so clearly through the Scriptures and they wanted to share what He had said. As we sat and listened, they told us that through something we had said a few weeks earlier God had begun to speak to them. Some time earlier, John and Rose had given Ray and myself an amazing personal gift to help support us in our work. They

were incredibly generous to us and we decided to put some of
that gift aside as a pension fund for ourselves for the future.
Throughout the years it had not been possible for us to put
money aside for our future, there had always been such
pressing needs, whether for ourselves, the team or for others
we met. When we were wondering where the £100,000 would
come from, we wondered whether we should try and cash in
some of the money they had given us.

When John and Rose had visited us, we had told them that
although we were not sure whether this was right, we wondered if they would mind us using some of the money they had
given us. They had replied that the money was ours and we
could do what we wanted with it. It was only a two-minute
conversation, however what we had said had really stuck in
their minds. They had thought to themselves, 'If Ray and
Nancy are prepared to give out of the little that they have then
surely we must go back to God and ask if we should give out of
what we have.' When they went back to God, He showed them
through Scripture that they should again partner with us in the
Caedmon project. They had come to tell us that if we were
prepared to give our bit, then they would give whatever it took
to complete the project. Praise God for people who listen and
respond to God's Word. God had done it – He had raised our
Lazarus back to life. What a fantastic God we have!

Our building project came to an end in April 2001. What a
celebration we had as we stood in the building with tears
pouring down our faces and remembered God saying all those
years previously, 'I am going to give you a missions and arts
complex.' We never ever imagined that God would take us on a
journey that would last five years and cost £3 million, and that
after we had learnt so many lessons He would provide a
building that would far surpass all that we had asked for or even
imagined (Ephesians 3:20). If you are ever in the area of Bristol
please do phone and make an appointment to see our little
miracle. It is a real testimony to God's incredible faithfulness.

During the writing of this book, God has begun to speak to
us about more 'territory' He has for us. He has again been

challenging us to 'hug God on the high wire', calling us to get up close and personal to Him, to listen to Him, and spend time in His presence because He has more territory He wants us to possess; more exploits He wants us to do. At present we are praying for God to bring three million souls into His kingdom through the work of ngm. We know this is a huge target, but if we can believe God for £3 million pounds, then we want to believe God for three million souls. We also believe God could be telling us that there is more territory for our base. One of our greatest needs at ngm is for accommodation. We are constantly being hampered by the fact that we have no place to 'house' people when they come to be trained, whether on a short- or long-term basis.

We have just heard that the land next door to Caedmon has being put on the market at around £1 million. It would obviously be ideal to have the land and then build an accommodation block right next to the training complex. At one of our midnight prayer meetings God again highlighted the fact that there is land that we have yet to take. We are right at the point where we need to hear God. Here we go again . . .

Exercises for your faith muscles

Read John 11:1–44 and answer the following questions.

▶ Take a few moments to think through how disappointed Mary and Martha must have been in Jesus. He was their special friend. They knew that if Jesus laid His hands on Lazarus he could have regained his health, but when they called Jesus He did not respond. In fact, even when Lazarus died Jesus did not turn up for the funeral. Has there ever been a time when God did not turn up when you expected Him to do so? What did that do to your faith?

▶ Mary and Martha did not allow their disappointment to stop them from continuing to trust in Jesus. It is so easy to allow disappointment, discouragement or disillusionment to destroy our trust in God. Think through/discuss ways in which we can overcome these things and triumph in our faith.

► Read Nehemiah 4. Nehemiah 4:1 tells us that Sanballat ridiculed the Jews for doing what God had told them to do. In Nehemiah 4:8 Sanballet again decided to stir up trouble for the Jews. What was Nehemiah's response to this? Write down/discuss what can we learn from this.

► Encourage yourself/each other by remembering/telling stories of God's faithfulness to you.

► Memorise Ephesians 2:8:

'For it is by grace you have been saved, through faith – and this not from yourselves, it is the gift of God – not by works, so that no-one can boast.'

H.O.T. Faith

What a joy it has been to write a book about God's amazing faithfulness. I have found while writing this manuscript that I have praised, prayed, wept and laughed about God's exuberant love towards us as I have recalled many stories from the past. At times I can hardly believe God's overwhelming grace towards us, His people. I have been inspired again to believe God for much more than ever before. I have realised afresh just how easy it is to get comfortable with where you are at so that before you know it you are living in the ordinary rather than the supernatural provision of God. The god of this world can so easily deceive us and have us believing in a small man-made god rather than seeing the truth of the One we serve. We serve a *huge big God* who is not bound by man-made restrictions – the King of kings and the Lord of lords. The One who created the universe with the words of His mouth. It is so good to know that even though He is a huge amazing God, He is also small enough to live in our hearts. A close intimate relationship with each of us is something He desires and longs for with every fabric of His being. As we run after God and pursue that depth of friendship, we will come into a place where we can begin to see our faith walk grow and develop.

God is looking these days for people who will live on the edge for Him. He is looking for people who will be prepared to give their all for His Kingdom. He is looking for people who although they feel totally inadequate and unprepared, will take up their crosses and follow Jesus to the ends of the earth. It does not matter how many successes you have or how many failures you encounter, what matters is that you are still walking with God and crying out for Him to take you deeper. God is looking for people who are hungry for the deep life. Are you hungry for God? Are you hungry for His Spirit? Are you unsatisfied with the ordinary? Then you are right on the edge of discovering a fresh, new, dynamic life of faith.

My prayer for you is that as you *hear*, *obey* and *trust* God, your red-hot faith will have a dynamic effect in your own life, throughout your family, friends, neighbours and the world in which you live.

> 'Lord, my prayer for those reading this book is that they will hunger after You in such a way that nothing will satisfy other than You. Lord, take them into a deeper and more intimate walk with You where they are able to hear and identify Your voice so clearly. Lord, I pray that each person reading this book will hunger after You in such a way that they will be prepared to obey whatever You say. Lord, I pray that they will then put their full trust in You and walk with You on the high wire. May the fire of Your Spirit so burn within them that the effect of their hot faith will be seen wherever they go. For I ask it in the mighty name of Jesus – Amen.'

ngm Information

Ray and Nancy are the directors and leaders of ngm (new generation music and mission). In 1980 God very clearly called Ray and Nancy to leave their home in Scotland and come to England to work as missionaries in the youth culture. During their first nine months of Christian work they founded and birthed in prayer the band/team ministry they called Heartbeat. Nancy was one of the singers and Ray was the drummer. Through the work of Heartbeat they literally saw thousands come to know God for themselves.

In 1985, God gave them a deep desire in their hearts for revival and a strong conviction that a new outpouring of His Spirit was going to take place in the nations of the world. During this time they also brought this prophetic message to millions of people as they released singles that broke into the mainstream charts. Heartbeat appeared on many radio and television shows including the BBC's chart programme *Top of the Pops*. As their ministry continued to develop, and in line with their growing vision to see a new generation reached for God, they changed their name in 1989 to ngm. With Heartbeat finishing in 1991, a new chapter had begun with God promising even greater blessing as they continued to bring the good news to this needy and hurting generation.

They now have over 120 full-time people in ngm working as missionaries to a needy and hurting youth culture not only in Britain but also abroad. They work in three main areas: church planting, media, and training. Artists include Andy Hunter,

Steve, Doug E. Ross, and T-girl. In 2001 they opened their new £3 million missions and arts complex which consists of two recording studios, one dance studio, an IT room, two programming rooms, several training rooms, and a performance venue, as well as a separate building for offices, seminar rooms and accommodation. They train people from the age of seventeen in evangelism, communication and their particular art form, whether it be singing, dancing, DJ-ing, playing an instrument or worship leading.

If you are interested in hearing how you can affect the youth culture of today, be trained in your art form, and learn how to live by faith; or if you would like more information about ngm or wish to receive regular newsletters, please contact us via the details below:

> ngm
> Caedmon Complex
> Bristol Road
> Thornbury
> Bristol
> BS35 3JA
>
> *email*: ngm@ngm.org.uk
> *website*: www.ngm.org.uk

Nancy Goudie's
Spiritual Health Weekend

Three exciting days to transform your walk with God

Would you like to be pampered physically and toned up spiritually?

Nancy Goudie's spiritual health weekends could be just the thing you are looking for!

Nancy Goudie runs a weekend conference at the beginning of February each year at a luxury four-star Marriott hotel in Bristol. The weekend is for ladies of all ages. Come and enjoy the excellent food and leisure facilities (spa, steam room, sauna, fitness room and luxury pool) and also experience God through the inspirational teaching and creative spiritual exercises from Nancy. Special guests include some of the talented ngm artists. Each conference is booked well in advance so please book early to avoid disappointment.

See page 190 for more information and booking details.

Further Information, Booking and Contact Details

For further information, booking and ordering please contact:

Nancy Goudie
ngm
Caedmon Complex
Bristol Road
Thornbury
Bristol
BS35 3JA

Tel: 01454 414880/2
Fax: 01454 414812
Email: nancy@nancygoudie.com

Or visit her website at www.nancygoudie.com

Should you wish to contact Nancy, be on Ray and Nancy's prayer letter list or join their group of intercessors, then do write to Nancy at ngm.

Books and Other Products by Nancy Goudie

Books

Spiritual Health Workout – Kingsway Publications, £6.99
This unique book is practical, accessible and fun to use and will help you exercise your faith muscles and tone up your heart for God.

50 Creative Worship Ideas – Kingsway Publications, £8.99
This is the last book in the series from Kingsway called '50 Great Ideas'. Nancy's book is packed with innovative, creative and fun ideas which are designed to help you explore more of the presence of God and the power of the Holy Spirit in our lives and in our church meetings. Ideal for small groups or large church events.

Both the above books are available from any Christian bookshop or direct from ngm or via the website:

www.nancygoudie.com

Bible reading planners

A superb way of systematically reading through the Bible in one or two years.

These can be purchased for 50p from ngm or via the website:

www.nancygoudie.com

Cassettes and CDs

Journey to the Cross – *Meditation Cassette & CD*, £9.99 & £6.99
A powerful CD and cassette that will take you to the foot of the cross to experience Christ's death and impact you with the amazing love of God.

A God Encounter – *Meditation CD*, £9.99
A unique meditative worship experience which will transport you into the very throne room of God.

Peace Like a River – *Meditation CD*, £9.99
If you have ever experienced stress, carried worries, fought fears, or are just looking for an oasis in your busy life, then this CD is for you. This recording will take you to a place of tranquillity where peace, love and grace are yours in abundance. Use this CD daily and you will find peace like a river flowing through your soul. The meditation experience is ideal for those who are not Christians as well as for those who are.

All the above music and meditation CDs and cassettes are available direct from ngm.